Wearing The Wind

First Lesson Sermons For Sundays After Pentecost (Middle Third) Cycle B

Stephen M. Crotts

CSS Publishing Company, Inc., Lima, Ohio

WEARING THE WIND

Library of Congress Cataloging-in-Publication Data

Crotts, Stephen M.
    Wearing the wind : first lesson sermons for Sundays after Pentecost (middle third), cycle B / Stephen M. Crotts.
        p.   cm.
    ISBN 0-7880-1385-8
    1. Pentecost season Sermons. 2. Sermons, American. 3. Bible. O.T. Sermons. 1. Title.
BV4300.5.C76   1999
252'.64—dc21
                                                                    99-32681
                                                                         CIP

For more information about CSS Publishing Company resources, visit our website at www.csspub.com.

Dedicated

to

Jim Glasgow —
a modern day Barnabas
who has made my coming to the Grove Church
joy, love, and faithfulness

Table Of Contents

Foreword

The Good Lord has called me to live at the water's edge. From my house I can see the marsh, the Intracoastal Waterway, and a barrier island with the Atlantic Ocean waves cresting and crashing upon it.

Living shore-side, one becomes immediately aware of the wind. Waterfowl ride its air currents. Nautical flags snap in the breeze. Whitecaps and ocean waves are driven by gales of atmospheric breath. Even sand dunes are sculpted by the wind.

I have been beckoned to the water in my small boat by a sea breeze on a hot summer day. I have been driven off the water by a nor'easter. And I have sheltered far inland from a hurricane. I have reveled in the marsh scented perfume of spring zephyrs, been lulled to sleep by soothing salt-sea laden wisps of wind, and thrilled to scything storm winds screaming at my door.

Yes, the wind and I are more than nodding acquaintances. We are related familiarly, but always on his terms. The wind never lets me forget he is boss.

Out on the slender peninsular where I dwell, nothing is more shaped by wind than the ancient oaks of the maritime forest. These moss-draped live oaks sweep upward in sun-reaching postures of adoration. And their branches are shaped by persistent and gusty gales. Sometimes graceful, at other times grotesque, the trees wear the wind as a habit.

Jesus, speaking to the man Nicodemus, told of the wind of God, "The wind blows where it wills, and you hear the sound thereof, but you do not know from whence it comes or whither it goes" (John 3:8).

As the wind shapes life by the sea, so the Holy Spirit shapes our lives in Christ.

These ten texts from Pentecost explain how.

Nothing is spared the Spirit's influence. He shapes our friendships, marriage, our love for our enemies, our heritage, sexual passion, wisdom, even our femininity and self-esteem.

Christians wear the wind of God. Like stately live oaks by the sea, God's grace and spirit make us conform to his image.

This book of messages explains but a wee portion of that phenomenon.

It is my prayer that you, rooted in Christ by faith, will yield to the shape of God's wind in your life as you live earth-side by heaven's fair shore.

Stephen M. Crotts
April, 1999
Somerset-By-The-Sea
Wilmington, North Carolina

Friendship?
Yes, Please!

2 Samuel 11:1-15

According to a recent poll only about ten percent of American males say they have a good friend. And while women fare somewhat better, neither do they set a record.

Why is this? I believe it is because we place such an emphasis on doing, producing, and having that we have very little time and energy left for developing relationships. In short, we'd rather have things than people.

Actually, the Bible predicts this is how it will be in the end of times. Revelation 18:11-13 describes the economy of Babylon, that quintessential city of sin. And it lists in order of priority the things her people value most. Gold is first on her list. Then follow such things as silver, linen, jewels, oil, and grain. And would you believe people are last on the list?

Revelation 21:1-21 describes the kingdom of God. And there, the economic priorities are exactly the opposite. People are mentioned first. And gold is mentioned last. It is used to pave the streets.

Clearly the typical friendless American male is more like a citizen of Babylon than he is the kingdom of our Lord.

A few years ago a lovely woman from Kenya worshiped with us for some time. Her name was Adihambo Otineo, which means "Beautiful Dawn." I asked her once if she liked it better here in the United States or back home in Africa. She grew quiet for some time. Her face worked with emotion. And finally she spoke with deep feeling. "I think I like it better in Kenya," she confided. "Here in the United States people are very busy and wealthy. And instead of giving you themselves they give you things. But in Kenya we are very poor. And we have nothing to give to one another but ourselves. But that we do give. And I miss the gift of people." God help us!

The late Dr. Francis Schaeffer once remarked that the true religion of the western world is not Christianity, but private peace and affluence, a really horrible value system that negates friendship. Consider: in our nation we value our privacy. Daniel Boone, several hundred years ago, kept moving west looking for "elbow room." And that same attitude is prevalent in our national psyche today. Witness the American automobile. It has killed the bus and train public transportation systems. And we're not even interested in car pooling. We just want our privacy. "Elbow room."

"Convenience" is another value in our national religion of private peace and affluence. We like our instant breakfast, drive-in windows, Instamatic cameras, and instant credit. Why, just use your razor and throw it away. The same with a writing pen, soda bottle, and mind you, a marriage. All for the god of "convenience."

I've only seen the previews, but the movie *Three Men and A Baby* seems to be about this very thing. Someone not wanting the trouble of a newborn infant leaves her child in a basket on the door step of three practiced bachelors. And the three men, adopting the child, soon realize that children, indeed — people in general! — are not at all convenient. So we instinctively avoid messy entanglements with others.

Beyond convenience and privacy is yet a third value we're really into today, and that is mobility. The average American moves every three years. Life is reduced to little more than a game of musical chairs. We don't want to be tied down. We live for the weekend, then take off! And there is very little time for real relationships to develop.

So the logical result of our values is a lifestyle that is friendless. We are little more than high tech human tumbleweeds passing our lonely way through life privately, affluently, with our things — our A/C, CD, VCR, Condo, and Z. For us there is no one, just our "stuff." We don't belong to a club, guild, union, clan, church, or league. Loners, floaters — we are.

And the Bible warns us this is all absurd. We were made for more! Why, in the Bible, the first negative statement God uttered was, "It is not good that the man should live alone" (Genesis 2:18). So God made us for relationships. He made us to love him and to love our neighbor as ourselves (Mark 12:29-31).

Think, if you will: Does not even our church building reflect this value? In the nave we learn to be friends with God in Christ as we worship. And then in the fellowship hall we learn to be friends with each other as we eat and talk, laugh and share and encourage.

In chapter 1 of Second Samuel, David learns of his good friend Jonathan's death. As youths they'd covenanted together trading cloaks and swords. They'd hunted and camped together, worshiped, traded stories, and suffered together the corrupt intrigues of King Saul's court.

Now Jonathan is slain in battle. And David grieves. "Very pleasant have you been to me; your love to me was wonderful, passing the love of women."

So adroit was David at cultivating friendship that his son, Solomon, commented on it years later in his book about wisdom. And this leads us to our second text. In Solomon's insight into the example his father set in relationships, he lays out the value of friends most succinctly.

Synergism

"Two are better than one," Solomon says. "For they have a good reward for their toil." Right away we are told that true friendships are a "toil." One has to work at it!

In American society today casual relationships are full of laziness and polite insincerities. "Friends" may pause briefly to chat as they pass on the street, but neither really hears what the other says about himself nor is either moved to any kind of meaningful response to the other. We hurry through our "Hello, how are you?" "I'm not too well." "Take care of yourself" conversations and move on. Like two ships passing in the night, we are prisoners in our own self-imposed solitary confinement.

The great people of God, though, always had their friendships. Elijah had his Elisha, Paul his Silas, David his Jonathan, and Adam

11

his Eve. Robert Peary, the first man at the North Pole, had his Matthew Henson. Mr. Bell, inventor of the telephone, had his Watson. Even singer Smokey Robinson had his backup singers, "The Miracles."

"I will make a help mate fit for you," God promises (Genesis 2). And so it is that the finest accomplishments of the human race are not done solo, but in the community of friends. We talk about Jesus and the twelve, a writer and his publisher, Neil Armstrong — first man on the moon — and his support crew, a coach and his team, a president and his congress, a doctor and his nurses. Fact is, life is a team sport. And it is in coming together that we find a power given to friendships that is denied the individual. Or as Solomon put it in the text, we find "good reward for our toil."

Example: Geese flying south for the winter leave the Hudson Bay in Canada and fly non-stop to the Chesapeake Bay. Using their famous V-formation they can achieve speeds of over fifty mph! Flying alone, however, a goose can only go half the speed and for hour and a half flights before resting. Why the difference between a flock and an individual bird?

Scientists point to a phenomena they call synergism. In formation, the lead bird breaks the air resistance creating in his path a helpful updraft for the birds who follow. When the lead bird tires, he drops back and allows another bird to lead. The others are pulled along in V-formation with a helpful wind suction. And scientists even believe that the incessant honking is a form of verbal encouragement to stay together, to keep up. Thus can birds accomplish more together than they can apart.

And this is what Solomon is observing in friendships. "Two are better than one because they have a good reward for their toil."

Encouragement

Solomon not only points us to the synergy of friendships, he also says that relationships provide us with much needed encouragement. "For if they fall," he writes, "one will lift up his fellow. But woe to him who is alone when he falls and has not another to lift him up."

I like the play on words in this portion of the text. At first it says, "if they fall." But then it kind of corrects itself and says, "when he falls." In life, you see, it is not really a question of *if* we shall fall but *when*. All of us sin. All of us get discouraged. All of us will grow disillusioned and want to quit. All of us will suffer confusion, fatigue, and bouts of depression. And the text says, "Woe be to anyone of us who is friendless when such a down time comes."

In today's world the friendless American male who is discouraged has to buy a friend by going to an analyst or he buys his fellowship at the bar, communing on highballs while tipsily telling his troubles to a stranger. But in Christ we have Christian friends and fellowship that offer so much more.

Jeremiah lived around 600 years before Christ. His name means "The Lord hurls!" Called to preach at age eighteen, Jeremiah was thrust into a forty-year ministry spanning the reign of a half-dozen kings of Israel. His message went largely unheeded. He was reputed to be a troublemaker. And in the end, when his nation was besieged and near collapse, his own people threw him into a miry pit. There wallowed Jeremiah — unheeded, rejected, thirsty, and depressed, But he was not friendless. The Bible says Ebedmelech the Ethiopian came and pulled him out and ministered to him.

That's what friends are for. In the down times when all the world goes out, a friend comes in. A smile, an arm around a shoulder, a phone call, a listening ear. With a friend, grief is halved, but joys are doubled.

Comfort

Next, Solomon says that friendship not only brings synergy and encouragement, it brings comfort as well. "If two lie together, they are warm: but how can one be warm alone?"

Perhaps Solomon is remembering his own father's death. King David evidently suffered from exposure. The Bible says he shivered and no amount of blankets could warm him. So they put another human being in the bed with him and he was warmed and comforted. In other words, more and more "things" could not comfort him. Only another person.

13

I'm thinking here of the comforting friendship that developed between Ruth and Naomi. Ruth was young, a widow, dirt poor, and hopeless. Yet she befriended her mother-in-law who was just as bad off as she was except she was old as well. "Entreat me not to leave you," Ruth urged Naomi, "for where you go I will go."

You'd think two such desperate people who find each other would end up a double drowning! But didn't Solomon say there was synergy and encouragement and comfort in friendships? And so it was that Ruth, in helping Naomi solve her problems, found that she also solved her own. Talking, sharing, dreaming, crying, hoping, scheming, and laughing with Naomi, Ruth's quality of relationships came to the notice of Boaz who asked for her hand in marriage.

Charles Dickens wrote, "No one is useless in this world who lightens the burden of it to anyone else." We get cold alone. But together we can stay warm. In coming to you for friendships I acknowledge I need you. I need your listening ears, your insight, your wisdom, your help. Alone I am weak and vulnerable. Together with you I find what I need to go on. Leslie Weatherhead wrote, "He who hugs life to himself loses all joy in living; he's lonely and self-excluded from joy. He who gives himself away to others shall find a fullness of life that will develop into the wholly satisfying life that is everlasting."

Trouble

Comfort, synergy, encouragement — these are what friends are for. And now this: trouble. Solomon writes, "And though a man might prevail against one who is alone, two will withstand him."

In the army the command to "dig in" means to dig a foxhole big enough for yourself and at least one other person. The idea is that if trouble comes at least we'll face it together.

So much of our private peace and affluent lifestyles today are spent running away from trouble and the responsibility to do something about it. Yet trouble has a way of nipping at our heels no matter how fast or far we run. Divorce. Emotional illness. Substance abuse. Financial reversals. Illness. Death. And unless we're "dug in" with a friend, the text says we'll not "withstand."

I asked an old man, "What is life's hardest burden?" And he answered, "To have nothing to carry."

This portion of the text calls us to get involved with others, to help them carry their burdens, withstand their adversaries, overcome their problems. That's what my favorite Old Testament character Jonathan did for David.

David was a young lonely shepherd boy when Samuel anointed him a future king. He later killed the giant Goliath with his slingshot, excelled as a poet and musician, and proved himself again and again on the battlefield. The women used to sing, "Saul has killed his thousands, but David his ten thousands!"

But there was a problem. King Saul grew jealous. And he tried to kill David. Fleeing into the desert, David lived a wanted man, hounded, often hungry.

That's when Jonathan befriended David. Now Jonathan was Saul's son, and as such, he was the rightful heir to the throne of Israel. Still, he accepted David's anointing by Samuel, so selfless was he. And the really beautiful thing is that Jonathan managed to balance his relationships with his tormented father and the fugitive David without being disloyal to either. In fact, he died on Mount Gilboa fighting the Philistines at his father's side. When David heard of his friend's death in battle, he mourned deeply. Jonathan had so loyally helped him out of so many tight spots. And now he was gone. And in 2 Samuel 1:17-27 David wrote his most beautiful poetic lament, "How are the mighty fallen ... The glory of Israel is slain upon the high places ... I am distressed for you, my brother Jonathan; very pleasant have you been to me, your love to me was wonderful, passing the love of women."

That's what friends are for.

In a world where the population doubles every 37 years or less, it is ironic that so many feel isolated, so alone these days. The stuff of good friendships is all about us, if we'll only heed the word of God and desire it and work at it. For all of the synergy, encouragement, comfort, and strength to face trouble awaits you in intimate relationships.

But let me do one thing more as I close. Proverbs 17:17 says, "A friend loveth at all times." And this friendship spoken of must surely speak of God. For, indeed, our earthly friends will die as Jonathan did, or they'll wed and pull away from us as Ruth did. But Jesus Christ alone can promise to love you at all times. "I will never leave you nor forsake you," Christ promises.

In Christ your life can have the synergy of the Holy Spirit, the encouragement of the promises of God, the comfort of eternal life, and the companionship of Jesus who will "dig in" with you to face life's troubles one at a time.

Solomon ends his testimony to companionship saying, "A three-fold cord is not quickly broken." Why not decide right now not to go it alone any longer. By repentance and faith in Christ braid your life together with God and some of his people. For —

"Two are better than one, because they have a good reward for their toil. For if they fall, one will lift up his fellow; but woe to him who is alone when he falls and has not another to lift him up. Again, if two lie together, they are warm; but how can one be warm alone? And though a man might prevail against one who is alone, two will withstand him. A threefold cord is not quickly broken."

How To Affair-Proof Your Marriage!

2 Samuel 11:26—12:13a

Country singer Gene Watson croons:

> *Slip into something soft,*
> *And then come slip into my arms again.*
> *Strip away your conscience and*
> *Take off your wedding band.*

Cheating has become America's national pastime. Statistically, 65 percent of men have affairs by age forty. For women it's 35 percent.

Talking with a pastor who had demitted the ministry due to sexual misconduct, he confided, "I never thought it could happen to me. But it did. For fifteen minutes of rolling in the sheets I sacrificed everything precious in my life — wife, children, reputation, ministry, even my health."

Another friend confided to me after adultery, "It just happened! It just happened!" I said, "No, it didn't just happen. You let it happen!" For in every affair there is a choice, steps taken, road blocks crashed, red lights run. For a very poignant look at the process that leads to an affair read 2 Samuel 6-12. There the anatomy of David and Bathsheba's affair is laid bare before one's eyes.

In walking through this epic story of wrong, I want to make my points with all *E*'s. The point is, an affair is *easy*.

Estrangement

The first step is *estrangement*. David and his wife Michal are on the outs. He is excited about bringing the Ark up to Jerusalem.

17

He has danced for joy. But Michal has belittled him. "My, how the king has lowered himself before the people today, dancing half naked like an ape!" From that day on Michal and David barely speak.

Most marriages that fail do so not from a blow out, but from a slow leak. We get into marriage with such high expectations. We're in love, choosing to act in one another's best interests. "Forsaking all others I will keep myself only unto you so long as we both shall live." Early marriage is exciting, and we pursue it with verve!

Then there is a fight, some disappointment, and resentment settles in. A slow leak.

As the poet has written, " 'Twas not love's going hurt my days, but that it went in little ways." The snap is gone. Sex becomes routine. She can't remember a tender time. He can't recall her support. So they quit trying together.

Two single men were talking. One remarked, "If I ever get married I want a wife who is an economist in the kitchen, a lady in the living room, and a bobcat in the bedroom." He did marry several years later, and his chum asked him if he got what he wanted in a woman. "Yes, but garbled," he replied. "My wife is a lady in the kitchen, a bobcat in the living room, and an economist in the bedroom."

Syracuse University has spent considerable time researching marriage. Of the ten most important things couples say they want in a marriage, sex is ninth. Caring, a sense of humor, and communication are tops.

Among men, the top five things they want in a wife are: (1) Respect. "She makes me feel capable." "She is proud of me!" "She is willing to follow my lead." (2) Domestic support. A home that is a refuge from the stress of the world. A home that's fun, pleasant, and tasteful. (3) Companionship. As in walks and talks, entering one another's world. (4) Sexual fulfillment. "She responds to me. She studies what is mutually pleasing, gets good at it, makes time for me, takes sex seriously." And (5) an attractive wife. She is clean, does her hair, cares how she looks, stays in the best shape she can.

18

Naturally, all of these values are constantly coming in and out of focus; but a good wife is always monitoring, adjusting, caring, trying. She keeps her marriage fresh.

So, if these are what a man wants of a wife in marriage, what then does a woman want of a husband? (1) Affection. The first thing Genesis 1-2 says God didn't make out of dirt is woman. Ephesians 5 explains that wives are made to be "cherished." This means romance, a steady stream of hugs, pats, compliments, kisses, and courtesies. At an airport, I saw a woman wearing a button that read, "This is my husband's idea of jewelry." Contrast that with William Jennings Bryan's hair over his ears. When asked why he wore it so since it was unfashionable, he said, "When I was courting my wife, she thought my ears stuck out funny and asked me to grow my hair long to cover them, so I did." To which his pal replied, "But that was years ago!" "Sure, " Bryan said, "but the romance is still going on!"

(2) Women want conversation on a "feeling" level, and (3) honesty and openness. Not sullenness. "A man who won't close the door on me." (4) Financial support. And (5) family commitment. Not a Dagwood Bumstead who passively sleeps and eats, but an active man who puts time and energy into the marriage, the children, the family.

On my wedding day, Joseph Paul Aiken, my grandfather, said to me, "Stephen, if you treat your wife like a queen, you'll get to be the king." He was paraphrasing the Golden Rule: "Do unto others as you would have them do unto you." Such does not come naturally. We have to work at it, strive to keep the marriage pumped up.

This is why happily married couples read, study, talk, ask, "How am I doing?" They listen, acquire role models, keep marriage among their top priorities. Without such action, the marriage develops a slow leak, until, like David and Michal, an ice age sets in. And they make the perfect couple. He's a pill! And she's a headache!

Encounter

So, David and Michal are estranged. Next in the anatomy of an affair comes the *encounter.*

19

King David is middle-aged. He's lost a step on the battlefield, so he stays home while the whole army marches to war. Having slept late, he broodily walks his patio, and from there spies his neighbor's wife, Bathsheba, immodestly bathing in her roof top garden.

Don Wharton, a friend of mine who is a songwriter and performer, told me other musicians constantly tell stories about how women throw themselves at them. Don said it never happens to him. He first thought he must be ugly or unsexy or something like that. Then he realized how in every one of his concerts he mentions his wife, how much in love they are, and sings some love song about her. Don realized how he is sending out signals to other women, "I'm spoken for." "No chance with me!" "I've got what I want!" His love for his wife simply jams women's radar.

Some experts believe man has a hormonal lack only his wife can provide with respect. And similarly, woman has a hormonal lack only her husband can provide with cherishing. If the spouse does not provide it, a hunger sets in. And according to 1 Corinthians 7:5, Satan will try to provide for it with an affair. This is what you have in the text. David is estranged from Michal, while Bathsheba's husband is absent, away at war. Both had pent up hunger. They were sending out signals of their lonely dissatisfaction. And they encountered one another.

Empathy

Estrangement. Encounter. An affair is so easy. Next comes *empathy*. Look at the action verbs in 2 Samuel 11:1-5. David *saw*. David *sent*. David *inquired*.

It used to be women were quite sheltered. They never went out in public without a chaperone. And only then with their hair up and veiled. Now, with women joining the work force, dressing to show off their figures, and their hair down, encounters are much easier.

So, two starved people meet, sparks fly in their looks, in a whiff of perfume, in a chance touch. In and of itself, these things are not bad. But if the sparks land in dry lives, then a flame is quickly kindled.

What we are talking about is a bonding, a meeting of needs between two people never meant to relate on such a level. A hand on the shoulder. Words like, "Sometimes I don't want to go home." "You have a nice figure." He volleys in her court. She responds. And, so, the two begin to flirt, to look for opportunities to be around each other. At the desk. On the phone. At the water cooler. Feelings sent. Feelings received. The hook is set. He makes her feel cherished. She makes him feel respected.

Enjoyment

David "saw from the roof a woman bathing; and the woman was very beautiful." The Bible says he enjoyed it and wanted more. So, "He sent messengers."

This is the adventurism, the flirtation, the infatuation of an illicit romance. The deceptive sweetness of forbidden fruit. Like a moth drawn to a flame, we fly closer. "I'll just carry her bags up to her hotel room. That's all." "I'll just stay ten minutes and leave. I can handle it."

We now begin to live in a fantasy world. We wonder how it would be. We undress them in our minds. Our thoughts are ripe with the pleasures of them.

Expedite

Romans 13:14 warns, "Make no provision for the flesh to gratify its desires." This is a road block we next crash quite brazenly. Estrangement. Encounter. Empathy. Enjoyment. And now, *expedite*. David actually sent for Bathsheba. And she came to his palace. It was like granting Satan an easement across his property.

We decide to go to a weekend business conference. She is there too. We arrange to stay in the same hotel. Go out to dinner together. Share a couple of drinks ...

Or we decide to ask her to work late at the office ...

"I'll just drive her home ..."

Bolder and bolder we become. "You have nice shoulders." "Why, thank you. I sure could use a back rub."

21

Expression

The next step is *expression*. The text says, "So David ... took her ... and he lay with her." They stepped over the line. Thoughts became action. Fantasy turned into sex.

Now the two adulterers become obsessed, totally addicted, so that they often lose all sense of judgment. Nothing else matters but to be together — not spouse, not children, not church, not reputation. She swills in the cherished feelings. He is inebriated with her respect.

In a nearby town, a certain banker was having an affair with his secretary. At lunch he would go out to his car backed against the shrubs, and stealthily climb into the trunk and close the lid. She would come out ten minutes later and drive the Cadillac out to a secluded wood where he would pop the trunk, climb out, and join her for an amorous time. Well, as fate would have it, she was low on gas one day, stopped at a filling station, and he, thinking they were at their rendevous, popped the trunk lid and climbed out, to an audience of laughing filling station customers and attendants. What fools adultery makes of us!

It's easy! Estrangement. Encounter. Empathy. Enjoyment. Expedite. Then Expression. And suddenly you're a fool!

Adultery is not purely a sexual sin. It is at its root the inability to deal with normal feelings of romance toward someone who was never meant to meet those needs. The problem is not *between* two people, but *in* two people. They will not nurture a relationship so that it lasts.

Effects

An affair is not over with the sexual experience, for there is one step further: the *effects*. Second Samuel 12:7-14 explains how Bathsheba became pregnant, how David murdered her husband, Uriah, and lived a coverup for a good year. "I can get away with it," David thought. "Nobody will have to know." Ah, but God knew! And he judged.

David and Bathsheba's child died, and Nathan the prophet said to David, "Because you have utterly spurned the Lord, the sword shall not depart from out of your house."

David's daughter, Tamar, was raped. His son, Ammon, was murdered. His boy, Absalom, rebelled and was slain. His next-in-line-for-the-crown, Adonijah, was killed. And Solomon wed over a thousand wives and they turned his heart away from the Lord. My, my! But what an awful legacy of immorality David thrust upon his children.

A man, utterly broken from the effects of adultery, once moaned to me, "If I had known how far down it would take me, how long it would hold me, how deeply it would hurt me, I would never have done it." Adultery is like a rat nibbling the cheese in a trap. The food is great. But the service is terrible. Just how terrible adultery can be is eloquently described in the following quote, written by the husband of an unfaithful wife.

"One reason it feels so good to be married is the sense of being chosen. Out of all the people in the world she chose me. Me to touch. Me to express intimacy. Me to share life's deepest sighs and groans.

"When I'm with her I keep thinking what a gift she is. I keep telling myself, 'No one else gets to see this, to feel this. This relationship is exclusively ours.' I feel confidence because I can please her, satisfy her. And when I wake up in the morning she's still in my arms. She brushes her hair back and smiles at me and soothes, 'I love you.' And I know all is right with my world.

"After she had the affair, I felt de-chosen. My entire confidence was shaken. Could I not please her? How could she take what was exclusively ours and give it to another? The thought of her in another's embrace, another man seeing her, holding her, inside her, left me so hurt, so confused, so suspicious, so angry, so emotionally eviscerated I wanted to die. But I wasn't even sure death could remove the pain. I still torture myself asking, 'Where did I go wrong? How did I fail her? Why was I not enough?' "

Shakespeare's *Othello* called being victimized by adultery, cuckolded. I call it the great betrayal. It's like taking two who've become one and making them a diluted three. Like walking with a rock in your shoe, adultery leaves a sharp object in your marriage bed, in your memory, in your loins.

"Now when I hold my wife I'm tormented by the thought she's comparing me with another lover. What used to be a mutual embrace of exclusive intimacy is now so much less."

Conclusion

A poll of 250 ministers who had had affairs discovered they only had one thing in common. They each thought, "It can't happen to me."

I once met Billy Graham. It happened to be during the televangelist sex scandals. My friend, Skip Stogdill, said, "Mr. Graham, thank you for all your years of purity in ministry. How is it you have managed to stay scandal free?" To which Mr. Graham replied, "It's because I constantly run scared."

And that's not bad advice for you and for me. Never say never! An affair is easy, all too easy. And it begins when we allow our own marriages to grow stale.

> *Drink water from your own cistern, running water from your own well. Should your springs overflow in the streets, your streams of water in the public squares? Let them be yours alone, never to be shared with strangers. May your fountain be blessed, and may you rejoice in the wife of your youth, a loving doe, a graceful deer — may her breasts satisfy you always, may you ever be captivated by her love. Why be captivated, my son, by an adulteress? Why embrace the bosom of another man's wife? For a man's ways are in full view of the Lord, and he examines all his paths. The evil deeds of a wicked man ensnare him; the cords of his sin hold him fast. He will die for lack of discipline, led astray by his own great folly.*   — Proverbs 5:15-23

How To Treat Your Enemies

2 Samuel 18:5-9, 15, 31-33

Did you hear about the man who went into the preaching ministry, worked for seven years, then resigned to go back to medical school and become a doctor? "People," he explained, "don't want spiritual health. They just want to feel good." But after working as a physician for seven years, he again resigned, this time to go back to school. "I'm going to become a lawyer," he explained, "because, in the end, people don't want spiritual health They don't even want physical health. They just want to get even."

I tell you, the world is like that: There is a growing surliness in our lives today. People are bristling with sarcasms, law suits, hand guns, and nuclear warheads. We are a people at war in our relationships. From our marriages to our child-parent relationships, to our next-door neighbors, to our work relationships and on beyond, we are a people doing combat.

And so much of our energy is consumed in licking our wounds and plotting our revenge. We want to hurt back, settle the score, get even.

Allow me to meddle in your lives for a few minutes by asking, "Who are you at war with? Who are your enemies? How have you been treating your foes?"

But you say, "I'm a Christian. I don't have any enemies." Come, come, now! Without enemies a person's Christian faith is highly suspect! Why, if you can live the truth in this untruthful world and not upset some pocket of evil, then you're probably not very salty or light-filled. Jesus, after all, didn't say, "You are the sugar of the earth." He called us "salt"! And salt has a way of

25

stinging. He called us "light" and light exposes. You can be sure that Christ had his enemies. So did Paul, Stephen, Peter, and others. In fact, Jesus said, "Woe be unto you when all men speak well of you" (Luke 6:26).

So, if you live for Christ, the question is not, "Will you have enemies?" The question is, "How shall you treat your enemies?"

And for those answers we turn to the life of David in 1 Samuel 25.

David has grown up watching his father's flocks near Bethlehem. He has killed the Philistine giant Goliath, been anointed the next king of Israel by the prophet Samuel, soothed King Saul with his music, become a military hero, and made his reputation as a poet with Psalm 23.

But now David's success has threatened King Saul. The man is jealous and he actually tries to kill young David. But David slips into the desert and hides out. Twice he has the opportunity to slay Saul, and twice he refuses.

Now David is driven to the edge of Israel. He is reduced to living in a cave. He is hot, thirsty, hungry, and lord of a band of renegades in search of survival. His enemy Saul is on the one side. His arch enemies, the Philistines, are on the other side. What David needs is a friend. But as we pick up the story in our text here, what David gets is another enemy.

Help!

In the text, David asks a Jew named Nabal for aid. You see, David has served as a kind of peace-keeping force in the area where Nabal lived. His military presence served as a wall against invasion or local mischief. And David saw to it personally that his men didn't bully Nabal's workers, steal from his flocks, or rape his women.

But now David needs a friend. He's at the end of his resources. And as the future king who has dealt honestly in the land, he sends his servants to the rich man Nabal asking for some supplies. He's not asking for what Nabal cannot give. He's only asking for what he desperately needs.

Be careful to note here that David has been completely honest with Nabal. He's even helped the man out by guarding his territory. So, now David is only asking Nabal to respond in kind, to do right by him. It's rather like an American tourist in Paris, France, today. The tourist, a former American soldier, helped liberate France in a war past. He has a right to ask some respect, some small return for his labors from the French.

Drop Dead!

So, David asks for help. And what did Nabal do? The text tells us Nabal was right in the middle of shearing his flocks. He was making money hand over fist! So, when David's servants visit and ask for aid, Nabal's mood turns nasty. He mocks them saying, "And who are you that I should help the likes of you? These days everyone is breaking away from Saul and pronouncing themselves king! No! I won't give you a single fig or a swallow of wine. Starve, you worthless scum!"

Has that ever happened to you? Do you know what it is to live righteously, to ask for your due and be so utterly spurned you despair of life itself?

I was sitting in the steam room at a health spa this week when a stranger in his mid-fifties entered. He sat down and began to tell me his troubles. For nearly 21 years he'd worked for a large textile industry. But his company had fired him last August just a few years before he could retire with full benefits. It seems the company didn't want to pay full retirement benefits, so they singled out those who'd be getting it soon, pressured them with relocations and impossible responsibilities, hoped they'd quit, but fired them for incompetency when they didn't.

No, the world has not changed all that much since Nabal sheared his sheep.

Revenge!

Back to the text. What's David going to do? He's done right. But he's been treated like an enemy. So David goes into what we might call a "slow burn." And when he gets hot enough, he tells several hundred of his men, "Strap on your swords." And they move to attack Nabal, to kill every man of his tribe before a day is out. They'll take what they need.

My, my! Can't we identify with David here? We've a hair-trigger when it comes to doing battle over our "rights." We find revenge so sweet!

An author named James Clark, while visiting a coastal book-store, found six copies of a 900-page boring historical novel on a bargain book table. The book was written by some other author who also happened to be named James Clark. So, he bought all six copies and mailed them to six of his enemies with the note en-closed, "I hope you enjoy this and won't mind the slight reference to you. James Clark." Ah! Sweet Revenge!

Then there's the one I read about in "Dear Abby." A divorcee wrote to say that her newly married ex-husband threw a big party at his home. And she was formally invited by mail being told to dress as for a masquerade party. She showed up dressed like a scarecrow and the maid ushered her into the ballroom where ev-eryone else was formally attired. Yes! Sweet revenge!

We humans are well-equipped for revenge. Why, we've de-veloped a huge stockpile of barbs, looks, ploys, law suits, cuts, and sword thrusts with which to get even.

Years ago, when former Soviet Premier Khrushchev was visit-ing a French cathedral, he remarked to a reporter, "There is much in Christ that is in common with us Communists, but I cannot agree with him when he says when you are hit on the right cheek, turn the left cheek. I believe in another principle. If I am hit on the left cheek I hit back on the right cheek so hard that the head might fall off." And so do we. And such was David's intent in the text.

Godly Advice

So, here comes David with 400 men. He's going to teach his enemy a thing or two. He's going to waste him!

It is interesting that Nabal's name in Hebrew means "fool." But fool that he was, the text tells us he had a beautiful wife of wisdom and discretion. Her name was Abigail, and she will for-ever be known as one of the great women in ministry.

Abigail, you see, learns of Nabal's foolish slight to David. So, she herself secretly gathers together the requested supplies and rides out to meet David. One person counseling forgiveness against 400 hot after revenge — that's the odds!

Well, Abigail meets David and, giving him the food, reminds him of several things. "Why stoop to your enemy's level by fighting with him? Your conscience is clear, your sleep peaceful. Let God take revenge. Keep your own hand from bloodguilt. And what is more, you are the future king. God will provide for your needs even if Nabal doesn't."

We all need to be reminded of those truths from time to time, don't we? Indeed, like David, we are quick to set off to avenge ourselves, and in so doing we rob ourselves of sleep, of a clear conscience. We lower ourselves to the level of our enemies.

Comedian Buddy Hackett said, "I've had a few arguments with people, but I never carry a grudge. You know why? While you're carrying a grudge, they're out dancing!" The truth is: revenge is a burden. Unforgiveness ends up hurting you worse than it does the other person. Hatred is like an acid. It ends up wounding the thrower more than it does the one on whom you throw it.

All this is what Abigail came out to remind David of. And this is what God would remind us of today. In Deuteronomy 32:35 God warns, "Vengeance is mine. I will repay."

Leave It To God!

So, what does David do? He's been slighted. His temper has flared. He's mustered the troops and gone out to get even only to bump into this woman who's brought him supplies and preached him a sermon.

What would you have done? There you are in front of 400 men. A woman with a message has stopped you. What would your troops think if you backed down?

But exhibiting a character that will forever make David a man after God's own heart, David hears God's word even from the lips of a woman, repents of his revenge, and sticks his sword back into his scabbard. "Like you say, lady. I'll turn it all over to God. The vengeance is all his. I'll let him judge between Nabal and myself."

There are many in our world today who point out that Christ's commands to go the second mile, turn the cheek, and forgive seventy times seventy are unworkable, impractical, in this dog-eat-dog world.

But what happens when David walks in this way? David starved, Nabal got fat, and King Saul lived happily ever after, right? Wrong! The text says Abigail shared plenty of food with David. Nabal heard of his wife's generosity and died of a heart attack. And David married Abigail. It's just like the Bible says in Proverbs 16:7, "When a man's ways please the Lord, he makes even his enemies to be at peace with him."

After World War I, President Woodrow Wilson as a Christian urged a greater measure of gentleness in dealing with the defeated nations. French Premier Clemenceau, who felt much more vindictive, objected, saying, "You talk too much like Jesus Christ." And so it was that a harsh revenge was meted out by allies on a fallen Germany. And the seeds were sown that led directly to World War II, a war which some historians say was really WWI fought a second time.

When will we ever learn Abigail's lesson? If we can trust our souls to Christ, can we not trust our enemies to him as well? Revenge fosters revenge. War breeds war. Getting even, one-up-man-ship, is a never-ending spasm of pain. And if you sow quarreling, you'll reap quarreling.

Take a lesson from the wise old mountain goats of Switzerland. Two "billies" meet on a high and narrow mountain path. The one is headed up and the other is headed down. And there is no room to pass. So, what do they do? Lower their heads and butt it out? That would most certainly send them both falling to their deaths below! So, here's what they do. One goat lies down on the trail and allows the other to walk over him. Then he gets up and passes safely on his way.

And that is what the gospel teaches for you and for me.

Conclusion

Yes, David treated his enemy Nabal with grace.

But notice in 2 Samuel 18:5, David had occasion to live graciously yet again. His own son, Absalom, had revolted, trying to wrest the crown for himself from his own father's head. The military coup had gone badly and now loyal troops were bearing down on Absalom. And, David, full of God's spirit of gentleness, urges his officers, "Be gentle with the young man Absalom for my sake." Life is so — daily. Enemies without and within assail us. And David's gentleness with his enemies blazes the trail for us all!

In Matthew 5:38-48, the Sermon on the Mount, Jesus says:

> *"You have heard it said, 'An eye for an eye and a tooth for a tooth!' But I say to you, do not resist one who is evil. But if anyone strikes you on the right cheek, turn to him the other also; and if anyone would sue you and take your coat, let him have your cloak as well; and if anyone forces you to go one mile, go with him two miles ... you have heard that it was said, 'You shall love your neighbor and hate your enemy.' But I say to you, love your enemies and pray for those who persecute you, so that you may be sons of your Father who is in Heaven."*

Then, in Romans 12:14 and following, the apostle Paul adds this:

> *Bless those who persecute you; bless and do not curse them ... Live in harmony with one another; do not be haughty, but associate with the lowly; never be conceited. Repay no one evil for evil, but take thought for what is noble in the sight of all. If possible, so far as it depends upon you, live peaceably with all. Beloved, never avenge yourselves, but leave it to the wrath of God ... No, "if your enemy is hungry, feed him; if he is thirsty, give him drink; for by so doing you will heap burning coals upon his head."*

Many of us think that by doing good to our enemies we drive them crazy trying to figure us out. We think this is the meaning of heaping "burning coals upon" their heads. Actually, there's a different truth here for us.

In ancient Palestine people heated their homes and cooked their meals with wood fires. And since there were no matches or "Bic" lighters or electric ranges, fire was a precious commodity. If it ever went out, it was difficult to get it going again unless you borrowed from your neighbor.

For this reason, when you went on a trip, you'd take some hot coals from your fire, place them in a firepot, sit it snugly in your turban, and go out on your journey. The warm embers kept your head warm, and when time came to camp for the night, you had enough hot coals to light your fire.

Furthermore, if you were visiting in my home and rose to go, I, as a hospitable person, would go to my fire, rake out a few glowing embers and heap them on your head (in the firepot, of course). This was a token of my hospitality, a winsome sign of my concern for your well-being.

And the Bible is saying this is the respect we should show our enemies. For, who knows the grace of God, but that our enemies can be turned into our friends. As Edwin Markham put it:

> *He drew a circle and shut me out,*
> *Heretic, rebel, a thing to flout.*
> *But love and I had the wit to win,*
> *We drew a circle that took him in.*

God Almighty, give me the grace to love my enemies. For Christ's sake.

You Can Create A Godly Heritage!

I Kings 2:10-12; 3:13-14

Former Colorado Governor Richard Lamm said: "Future historians will see best the multiple factors that led to the decline of America. But I suggest one of the major factors will be the failure to replace ourselves with enough stable children born to families with the ability to raise successful children."

What Governor Lamm is talking about is heritage and our failure to receive it, embrace it, enrich it, and transmit it. Thousands of years ago the prophet Jeremiah observed that his own people had loosened their hand from their heritage, let it fall and shatter. And it looks like we are doing the same. So, today, let's pause and look to Christ, our own heritage, and our own grip on things.

What Is A Heritage?

First of all, what is a heritage? In the text the Hebrew word for heritage means "something occupied, a possession, inheritance, estate portion, or heirloom." Basically, a heritage is something that remains after you, something you pass down to future generations. First Kings 2:10-12 explains how King David ruled forty years in Israel. His son Solomon inherited a rule from his father that was "firmly established."

When the sun sets, it does not suddenly grow dark. There is an afterglow in the clouds, at times very beautiful. And when we die, we do not suddenly cease to exist on earth. There is an afterglow of influence. And that influence is our heritage.

A heritage can be spiritual and take the form of God-fearing habits we've passed along to others. It can be intellectual in the

33

form of education. It can be emotional — good self-esteem, music appreciation, security. It can be a willful legacy — discipline! It can be physical — good looks, health, wise dietary habits. And our legacy can be material — houses, land, money, and the like.

The fourth commandment in Exodus 20:4-6 teaches that the heritage we engender can affect people in our family to the third and fourth generations. Just stop and consider how many people that is. If I wed and have three children and so on through four generations, there will be nearly 200 people in my immediate legacy. That makes you and me quite the pastors of prosperous flocks! Actually, Exodus 20:6 says your faithfulness can bless literally "thousands."

Take Abraham as an example. A simple desert shepherd was told by God, "Look toward the stars. So shall your descendants be" (Genesis 12). And so it is that we ourselves should be careful how we live. For we, too, are creating a legacy that will affect the lives of hundreds of people as yet unborn.

A Bad Example

With this in mind, let's take a moment and look at some examples of bad heritages.

The book of Ruth introduces Elimalech, the head of a Jewish household that included wife Naomi, and two young sons. During a time of severe famine and judgment, Elimalech, whose name in Hebrew means "My God is king," actually left Israel to live in present-day Jordan. There his two sons married foreign wives. Then Elimalech died. And soon his two boys died also. Thus he left a wife both widowed and bereft of her two sons as well. Not much of a heritage!

Then there is King Hezekiah's legacy described in 2 Kings 20:1-19. Hezekiah began to reign when he was 25 years old. The Northern Kingdom had already been destroyed by Assyria. And now Jerusalem and Judea stood alone as a remnant. The young king feared God, took Isaiah as his prophet, and began to reform Israel. For 29 years he reigned. But late in his life he grew lax and materialistic and his heart was not true to the Lord. God told Hezekiah that his kingdom would collapse after his death and that his sons would be enslaved and castrated by the Babylonians. And what was the king's response? He said, "Why not, if there will be peace and security in my days?"

Then there is the heritage of Eli described in 1 Samuel 1-4. Eli, whose name means "Uplifted," had two sons, Hophni and Phineas. Eli as high priest wanted his sons to follow in his steps. He'd enjoyed the privilege of tending the ark of the covenant at Shiloh, had ministered to Hannah in the temple, and even helped train Samuel, the first prophet. Yet all the while Eli's sons were blaspheming God and he did nothing to restrain them. Eventually they died in battle carrying the ark. Eli, you see, was so busy getting Israel ready for his sons that he forgot to get his sons ready for Israel.

Christian Life magazine went back to the records of 1677 and traced the genealogy of an immoral man who married a prostitute. 1,900 descendants resulted from that union. Of these, 771 were criminals. Two hundred fifty were arrested for various offenses. Sixty were thieves. Thirty-nine were convicted murderers. Forty of the women were known to have venereal diseases. These people spent a total of 1,300 years behind bars. They cost the state nearly three million dollars. As Proverbs 10:7 teaches, "The name of the wicked will rot ..."

Did you hear about the man riding a bus? A fellow passenger accidentally stepped on his foot and was foully cursed. After that the man began to complain loudly that the bus was too cold. And when the bus became crowded, he refused to stand up and give his seat to a lady. When his stop came and he got up to exit, the bus driver looked at him and said, "Sir, you left something behind!" "What?" the man said. "I've got everything I came with!" "No," the driver said, "you've left something behind. A bad impression."

So many die and leave a bad impression. As Jeremiah 2:7 says, we've made our "heritage an abomination."

A Good Example

Now some examples of a good heritage.

Certainly King David was not a perfect man. His coveting, adultery, murder, and lying show us that no heritage is untainted

35

by sin. But still David was "a man after God's own heart." That's because he could repent. And such pleases God.

King David has left us an example. His biography is included in the Old Testament. His poetry fills the book of Psalms. And among his children was Solomon.

To David God promised a heritage, that there would not fail to be a descendant of his to sit on Israel's throne forever. And so it was that Jesus Christ was born to us through David's line.

J. S. Bach is another example of a good heritage. A Christian, Bach lived in Germany in the late 1600s and early 1700s and worked for the church as a musician and composer. He fathered twenty children and his descendants dominated western music for 200 years. And even today his legacy enriches our lives as we listen to his works.

Then there is the Edwards family. *Christian Life* magazine traced the genealogy of a Christian man and woman who wed in the late 1600s. Three generations later Jonathan Edwards was born to become a revival preacher and president of Princeton University. There are 1,344 descendants in the Edwards legacy. Of them, 186 were ministers. Dozens were college professors. Eighty-six were state senators. And there have been three congressmen, thirty judges, and one vice-president of the United States. All this, and there is not one record of an Edwards in prison, divorced, or on public welfare. As Proverbs 10:7 says, "The memory of the righteous is a blessing."

What If Your Heritage Is Bad?

So, we've looked at what a heritage is, studied examples of both a bad one and a good one. Now let's ask, "What if the heritage you and I have received is a poor one?"

The psalmist said, "The lines have fallen for me in pleasant places, yea, I have a goodly heritage" (Psalm 16:6). But what if the lines have not fallen for you in pleasant places? Henry Ward Beecher said, "The first thing a man should do if he would succeed in life is to pick a good mother and father to be born of." But what if your parents have been ungodly?

The Bible teaches that our heritage can be cursed. Exodus 20:4-6 warns that this curse can come from as far back as your great-grandfather. Things like the occult, idolatry, divorce, substance abuse, and materialism can foully curse one's descendants. The prophet Ezekiel put it this way, "The fathers have eaten sour grapes and the children's teeth are set on edge" (Ezekiel 18:2).

We parents can bless or scar our heritage. Generations as yet unborn to us can be cursed or redeemed because of our choices. And so many of us have been victimized by our heritage. In Jeremiah 12:8 a Jewish man complains, "My heritage is like a lion in the forest." He feels devoured by his lineage.

Yet we do not have to limp on with the curse of a godless heritage, die, and pass the rot on to yet another generation. The curse can be broken, the chains broken, and a new heritage begun. God says, "I will again have compassion on them, and I will bring them again each to his heritage and each to his land" (Jeremiah 12:15). The Bible says, "Whatsoever is born of God is a new creation. Old things are passed away. Behold, all is brought into newness of life."

How can this be? Jesus has given his disciples a ministry of binding and loosing (John 20:23). And the fact is, by his authority we can remove the curse that clouds our legacies. So, though one cannot do anything about the heritage handed down to him, one can do everything about the heritage he hands down to others.

Building A Godly Heritage

All this brings us to the final point, a final question: "How can I create a godly heritage?"

Psalm 61:5 says, "Thou hast given me the heritage of those who fear thy name." A good heritage begins when one begins to acknowledge God, to reverence Jesus Christ, to stand in awe of his holiness.

Next come vows, commitment. Psalm 61:5 teaches, "For thou, O God, have heard my vows." And the result, he says, is to receive a godly heritage. It does no good trying to live the Christian life without commitment. And public vows and accountability in fellowship can certainly help foster maturity.

Then there is this word of God. Psalm 119:111 says, "Thy testimonies are my heritage forever; yea, they are the joy of my heart." A good heritage begins with the fear of God, commitment, and making God's testimony, the Word of God, one's blueprint for living. It's really simple to sum it up — "Trust and obey, for there's no other way, to be happy in Jesus, but to trust and obey."

And what are the results of this reverence for Christ? A godly heritage, an afterglow that blesses your children! Psalm 127:3 says, "Lo, sons are a heritage from the Lord, the fruit of the womb a reward." And did you realize that even single people can have spiritual sons and daughters? The single Paul spoke of "My child, Onesimus, whose father I have become" (Philemon 10).

In 2 Timothy 2:2 Paul urges Timothy, "And what you have heard from me before many witnesses entrust to faithful men who will be able to teach others also." He speaks of four generations of ministry here, reminding us that we each can bear a spiritual legacy of children for generations to come!

Certainly Paul, single as he was, developed a Christian heritage that matched his words. Timothy, Silas, John Mark, Onesimus, even the Praetorian Guards were a part of his legacy. And even his letters became the book we call the New Testament. What a heritage!

But the results of trusting and obeying Christ are not just an afterglow of heritage in children. It also includes possessions. Psalm 135:12 talks about "land as a heritage." And what a joy it is to be able to give our descendants a good head start in education, housing, and the like. Such is an inheritance of the Lord.

Church can also be an inheritance. Micah 7:14 commands us to "shepherd thy people with thy staff, the flock of thy inheritance." A righteous man leaves a good church for his children to dwell in.

Success is also the promise of a godly legacy. Isaiah 54:17 says, "No weapon that is fashioned against you shall prosper, and you shall confute every tongue that rises against you in judgment. This is the heritage of the servant of the Lord..." And there is even the promise that a goodly heritage is ripe with witness. In Jeremiah 3:19 God says, "I thought how I would set you among my sons, and give you a pleasant land, a heritage most beauteous of all nations, and I thought you would call me, 'My Father,' and would not turn from following me."

All this is in the heritage of the Lord!

Conclusion

Look to your heritage, my friend. None of us lives or dies to himself. For what we become and what we do will affect those who live in our afterglow.

In William Shakespeare's play *Twelfth Night*, the very capable and single Olivia shows no interest in relationships, in establishing a legacy among God's people, and an elder chides her for her selfishness and shortsightedness, saying, "To take such grace to the grave and leave no cup" is a crime of shame.

What about you and the cup of grace you hold in Jesus Christ? Will you leave the sweet wine of a goodly heritage in your cup for others to drink?

How Good
News Spreads!

1 Kings 8:(1, 6,10-11) 22-30, 41-43

In 1971 I made a trip to Russia. I was studying literature in England and hitched on to a discount side trip in November. Of special interest to me was the Russian author Leo Tolstoy. I had read his *War and Peace, Anna Karenina,* and *Resurrection.* Knowing of his Christian faith as well as his literary ability, I was drawn to all things Tolstoy.

You can imagine my joy in visiting Bright Glenn, Tolstoy's country estate. Some of his original manuscripts were stacked in a corner. One, then, could leaf the pages, scrutinize his penmanship, observe his strike overs. I sat at his desk, in his chair, even held his quill pen in my hand. I even fantasized that Leo himself walked into the room, greeted me heartily, and asked me to work with him on his newest novel!

That would be some invitation, wouldn't it? To co-labor with Tolstoy. A commission to co-author the latest Russian classic!

But, alas, there was no risen Tolstoy, no voice of commission. Only silence broken by the shrill November winter winds sweeping across the Soviet plains. And to this day I remain an uncommissioned artist.

There is in my life and yours, however, a genuine commissioning that, if you think about it, far outshines any other possible call to art. It is the Great Commission of Jesus Christ. "Go," God commissions in Matthew. "Go therefore and make disciples of all nations...." In 1 Kings 8:42, it is said of God, "Men will hear of your great name and your mighty hand and your outstretched arm." God, it seems, wills to work with us to create a people for himself.

Genesis 1-2 explains how the Lord creates the heavens and the earth and all life to enjoy it. Then on the seventh day God rested. Somewhere in time humanity sinned and all of life fell to ruin. But God rolled up his sleeves and went to work with a divine redeeming strategy that spanned the years and ultimately included Christ, the cross, the resurrection, and the indwelling power of the Holy Spirit.

This makes today theologically the Eighth Day of Creation. The Lord is at labor setting this abnormal world right again. And God invites us, he commissions us, to co-labor with him in this divine enterprise.

Now, just how is it that, as the text says, "Men will hear of your great name and your mighty hand and your outstretched arm"? Historically, there are four means of fulfilling the Good Lord's plan.

Voluntarily Going

The first is when God's people voluntarily go. Acts 13:1 and following speak of the early church in Antioch. A great host of people had learned of God's love in Jesus and embraced God by faith. A vital church community had formed and matured in knowledge, relationships, and ministry skills.

It was then that the Holy Spirit spoke, reminding the church that there were others "out there," in other cities, in other nations, on other continents that knew not of God nor his ways in Jesus. So it was that Barnabas and Paul were called on to depart the church voluntarily and carry the gospel to regions afar.

The early church didn't hoard the good news. It shared it with breathless excitement. And it did so by sending two beloved men — active, proven, and mature.

In the past, the modern church has sometimes been slack in sending missionaries. And when we do get around to doing so, we all too frequently send under-trained, immature misfits. More than I care to remember, I have seen untested men, unuseful here, discontented with job, see the mission field as an answer to boredom, a chance to flee their problems, to live the great adventure. And with self-will they head for the third world! And, sadly, their ministry on the field was as big a bust there as it was here.

I spoke with a national pastor in Nepal about missionaries the church sends out. He said, "If you won't miss them, don't send them to us!"

The early church sent Paul and Barnabas. They sent their best! We should do no less.

I recall Michael Murray, a bright young freshman at Duke University. He hardly missed a service in the church. He came early and stayed late mixing in with people. When we were short a song leader at the college ministry, he jumped in with his guitar for a whole year. He worked a six-month internship for the church to learn preaching and administration. He got a masters in linguistics. He made numerous short-term mission trips to China. He married a nurse willing to live in the foreign field. God built Michael very thoroughly. And one cold winter's Sunday night we went as a church out on the front lawn. There Michael and Yolanda Murray knelt down and we laid hands on them, sending them out to far regions. That was fifteen years ago. And the Murrays are preaching and living grace among a needy people still to this day.

Involuntarily Go

The gospel spreads when we volunteer to go. It also spreads another way — when we involuntarily go.

When Babylon conquered Israel in battle, the year was around 588 B.C., thousands of Jews were deported 500 miles east as slaves. In their captivity they carried their knowledge of God with them. And many a Gentile thus learned of the Lord.

Psalm 137 was written during this exile. Hear their lament as Jewish slaves living in a pagan land. "By the waters of Babylon, there we sat down and wept, when we remembered thee, Zion. On the willows we hung up our lyres. For there our captors required of us songs ... how shall we sing the Lord's song in a foreign land?"

There have been many led against their will to foreign lands. But they went with Jesus and evangelized the people to whom they were brought captive.

A Welshman named Sucant was abducted by pirates in 403 A.D. The sixteen-year-old Christian lad was taken to Ireland and enslaved for five years by the cruelest of Irish chieftains. Eventually Sucant escaped to join a monastery in Southern France. There he changed his name to Patrick, and intended to live out his years in the orderly monastic life of a monk.

Yet in 432 A.D., at the age of 45, the Holy Spirit called Patrick to return to Ireland and carry the gospel to his former tormentors. This Patrick did, investing the remainder of his life in the Irish. During the next 31 years he baptized more than 120,000 people into Christ!

Still today the Irish say of Patrick, "He found Ireland all heathen. He left it all Christian."

Voluntarily Coming

So, according to our text, "Men will hear of your great name." And how shall this be? As we go willingly or unwillingly to the nations.

Yet this is not all! For there is still a third way good news spreads, and that is as others voluntarily come to us.

First Kings 10:6-7, 23-24 tells of the Queen of Sheba traveling from Africa to Jerusalem to meet King Solomon. Fascinated by his religion and wisdom she came to soak it all in. "And she said to the king, 'The report was true which I heard in my own land of your affairs and of your wisdom, but I did not believe the reports until I came and my own eyes had seen it; and behold, the half was not told me.' "

Roman soldiers on duty in Palestine, men like Cornelius, willingly came to serve in war. While there they inquired of the gospel (Acts 10).

Here in the United States today foreigners are coming in droves to attend our colleges. They are the brightest and best of China, Zimbabwe, Australia, Russia, the Sudan, and beyond. Not counting diplomats, spouses, children, and business travelers, foreign students number well over half a million souls. Eighty-seven percent return to their nations upon graduation. Most assume positions of leadership. And they take with them so much of what they learned here.

Over the nine years I led a Bible study on Elon College's campus I met and had in my home youth from Holland, Israel, Peru,

Iran, and Germany. I tell you, the world is coming to our doorstep and we have opportunity to serve them. Perhaps many will convert to Christ and go home like the Queen of Sheba, saying, "Behold, the half of it wasn't told me! For, indeed, there is a God in Jesus Christ!"

Involuntarily Come

So, we may willingly or unwillingly go. But the gospel also spreads when we willingly come. And, finally, there is a fourth means of missions: unwillingly coming.

Paul the apostle was imprisoned for his faith. Yet in jail he evangelized and mentored soldier converts and wrote many of the New Testament epistles.

African tribes fought in the 1600s. Those defeated were delivered to Muslim traders who sold them to coastal slave merchants bound for North America. Bad as this all was, many a slave became a Christian. And the gospel has flourished.

I know of a Christian in Brazil thrown into prison on unjust charges. At first he fought to extract himself from such a hell hole. He was unwilling to come to such a place! Then God opened his eyes and he saw 4,000 men with him in the dungeon. And he began to testify and minister. Today, after eleven years in prison, his ministry is fruitful beyond what one can imagine! And no one else could have even gotten into the jail to bring such light! "Things turn out for the best for those who make the best of the way things turn out," he says.

Conclusion

If you study the history of missions, you find a big push in the early church to evangelize the Mediterranean world between 40 A.D. and 350 A.D. And they did it without radio, television, fax machines, church buildings, cars, phones, and huge budgets.

By 350 A.D. the church had stagnated and grown comfortable in the world. Come 500 A.D. Christianity was actually shrinking in number.

That's when Islam began to spread across Asia, Europe, and Africa. By 700 A.D. it looked like Muslims would rule the world! It was a dark age.

Slowly, however, the church began to reawaken. In 1492 Columbus encountered the New World. In 1517 Luther began the Protestant Reformation. And by 1600 the Colonial era began.

Up until then Christianity had been only a Western religion. But now it leapt to a global faith as missionaries carried the gospel to China, India, South America, and beyond.

Schools like Dartmouth College in New Hampshire were founded to evangelize Indians. They took John the Baptist's motto as their own, "A voice crying in the wilderness."

Still today, however, there are unreached peoples. Fully one half of the world's population hasn't heard the gospel.

In 1930 an American Christian missionary to Japan wrote home to his church alarmed about Japanese militarism. He pleaded, "Send me 2,000 of your best sons as missionaries or in ten years send me 1,000,000 men as soldiers."

It's chilling, isn't it? If we do not willingly go, God may send us unwillingly.

Make no mistake. God's middle name is "Go." We have been commissioned! As the text says, "Men will hear of your great name!" And by our going and their coming the world will know.

Let this be our truth: that Jesus is the Savior of the whole world. And he is our Lord.

And some of us must go.

Some of us must let go of our sons and daughters and friends. Others must help go with prayer and funding.

But all of us must get going!

For we've a story to tell to the nations!

Godly Sexual Passion For An X-Rated World!

Song of Solomon 2:8-13

The Hebrew word for love, *awhab* or *awrag,* means "to pant, to long for, to breathe heavily after." Psalm 41:1 says, "As a deer *pants* for the waters so my soul *longs* after you." In John 3:16, the idea is that God so loved the world, so breathed heavily after you and me, that he gave his only Son....

God is passionate for you. His breathing is labored. He loves you.

There is a book in the Old Testament that is full of heavy breathing. It is titled, "Song of Solomon," or "The Song of Songs." And it deals forthrightly with sexual passion, courtship, and matrimony.

King Solomon, the author, wrote 3,000 Proverbs and 1,005 songs (1 Kings 4:29-32). But this song is his best. In verse 1:1 it is called "the song of songs." That is a Hebrewism, a way of saying this song is his greatest hit. You will recall how Scripture labels Jesus the "King of Kings," meaning the King above all others. Likewise, this is Solomon's finest tune, his song of songs.

In the Old Testament there are three forms of literature. First is history, which includes Genesis to Nehemiah. Second is wisdom literature, which is found in the Psalms, Proverbs, Job, Ecclesiastes, and the Song of Solomon. Then there is prophecy, which encompasses Isaiah to Malachi.

Solomon's song is found in the wisdom literature section. Notice carefully the order in which it is included. There are the Psalms — 150 Jewish worship songs about our longing to know God. There follows Proverbs — 31 chapters on the human struggle to live usefully among people. Then comes Ecclesiastes — the

47

most cynical of the biblical canon. It is as if the struggle of the Psalms and Proverbs has left the devotee exhausted, depressed, and feeling overwhelmed with the futility of life.

Now any English major or storyteller of merit will tell you, after that much intensity, it's time to lighten up. Some comic relief, some serenity, some oasis of refreshment is sorely needed. Hence the scholars who gathered the Old Testament writings and placed them in order put the Song of Solomon after Psalms, Proverbs, and Ecclesiastes. For in a world struggling to relate to God and people, struggling with the cynicism and futility of life, there is the love between a man and a woman.

Warning! Jewish fathers will not allow their children to read this book. It is so absolutely graphic they rightfully fear it might stir their teenagers up with sexual passion!

Tony Evans, the one-of-a-kind Black gospel preacher, says, "I'll tell you what the Bible says about sex. If you're single, you can't have any. If you're married, then shop till you drop!" The Song of Solomon is the shop-till-you-drop book of the Bible.

See the benevolence of God here? The good Lord didn't just give us our sexual passion like a hand grenade. "Here! Fiddle with this until you figure it out!" Instead, God gave us an instruction manual.

I was teaching on sexuality at the College of Charleston in South Carolina. We were reading a particularly steamy passage out of Solomon's song, and I noticed a young man close his Bible, turn it over, and look at the spine to see if he really was reading from the Bible! Believe me, this is hot stuff!

Of a truth, Solomon's song is difficult to understand. After all, it is a poem. It is a love song. And it is 3,000 years old!

Imagine scholars 3,000 years from now trying to comprehend one of our hit love songs:

> *Be-bop-alula, she's my baby!*
> *Be-bop-alula, I don't mean maybe!*

So the Song of Solomon is a romantic poem, meant to be sung. It is a hit tune from 3,000 years past.

Biblical interpreters have wrestled with this song's meaning for centuries. Probably this is why we ministers shy away from preaching from it. Yet, in all this, three major interpretations have emerged over time.

Allegory

The first is allegory.

The Bible explains that history began with a wedding in a garden (Genesis 2). Jesus launched his public ministry at a wedding in Cana where he worked his first miracle by turning water into wine (John 2:1). Afterward, Jesus began to refer to himself as a groom with the church his bride (Matthew 9:15). And Scripture teaches in Revelation 19 that history will end soon at the wedding supper of the Lamb when Jesus comes for his church.

In Ephesians 5, Paul calls marriage "a great mystery." He explains that married love is a picture of God's love. It is an earthly example of a heavenly reality.

With this in mind, see how the maiden in Solomon's song begs her suitor, "Do not gaze at me" (1:5-6). Her complexion is ruined by the sun and hard work. This is interpreted as sinful man, ruined by the world, fearful of the Holy God's stare.

But in 5:11, the maiden's fears are calmed. She is in love and admiring her suitor's body. "His hair is ... black as a raven," she exudes. Yet if you look in Revelation 1:14, Jesus' hair is white. What lies between the Song of Songs and Revelation is the cross.

I once knew a mother with lovely brown hair. When her husband and daughter were killed suddenly in a traffic accident, her hair turned white overnight. Stress can do that to you. And if you allegorize Solomon's song, the stress of redemption's cross has changed Jesus, the lover of our souls. His raven black hair is now white as snow.

There is a communion scene in chapter 7:1-2. So very intimately he says to his bride, "Your navel is a wine glass filled to overflowing. Your body is full and slender like a bundle of wheat."

Now as the allegory concludes, the lovers stroll off together hand-in-hand. She's no longer afraid of him, insecure over her complexion. "My darling, I am yours, and you desire me. Let's stroll through the fields" (7:10-11).

Love Triangle

A second interpretation of the Song has it as a failed love triangle.

First Kings 2 tells us Solomon had a harem of over 1,000 wives. Some were wives he'd taken in the custom of the time to seal a military alliance. Others were taken as gifts to satisfy the ego of a visiting king. Convenience wives, territorial wives, the product of political expedience.

All this, then one day Solomon spied the lovely Shulamite maiden working in the fields. And he was smitten! So he sent and wooed her with gifts, poetic words, and all the peacockery a king could muster.

But, alas! She was in love with a simple shepherd. And she spurned Solomon's love for her, choosing instead her own man, a commoner.

Hence, the song's refrain, "Love cannot be bought, no matter what is offered" (8:7).

Nuptial Poem

The third interpretation of Solomon's love song understands it as a nuptial poem. A celebration of the sexual union between husband and wife.

I can see seven snapshots, seven "Kodak moments," as it were, in the love poem. There is the couple married and looking back on what first attracted them to one another. There is their courtship and romance, their wedding ceremony, the honeymoon — and let me say, it sizzles with purity and passion! Nothing is more erotic than two virgins coming together in Christ on their marriage night. Hollywood has never dreamed such a love scene! Next comes a quarrel and the struggle to make up. And finally there is the commitment to see the marriage through till death do us part.

Conclusion

I believe the Song of Solomon is a book for this generation. I believe it has been overlooked long enough. I believe the voice of

God can speak to us in our misery, in our dysfunction, in our alienation, through the eight chapters of this ancient song.

Many ask me how someone like Solomon, married over 1,000 times, can have anything to say morally about relationships. And my answer is, "Hey! Who better to speak to this incestuous, fornicating, homosexual, pornographic, adulterous, divorcing, lonely, agonizing generation than a man who'd been there, done that, and seen it, and yet come through it to meet Almighty God and grow wise and write his findings?"

Earnest Hemingway wrote, "In the end life breaks us all. But then we're strong in the broken places." Solomon, so broken, so wayward, so dysfunctional, yet so strong in the broken places, is now our author, our mentor, our teacher in God's benevolent provision.

If you are single and feeling lonely and left out — this book is for you.

If you are a teenager wrestling with your passions — this book is for you.

If you are married, trying to make it work — this book is for you.

If you are divorced — victimized by abuse, or victimizing others with your general human cussedness — this book is for you.

Read it.

At best you'll meet Jesus, someone who chooses you, loves you, transforms you.

At the very least you'll see how a relationship works, how marriage can be a little bit of heaven on earth, a foretaste of glory divine!

All Mine To Give!

Proverbs 22:1-2, 8-9, 22-23

Do you ever get tired of giving? Have you ever seriously considered dropping out of the ranks of tithers? I have.

Sometimes I get so overwhelmed by those computer generated appeal letters that come into my office, three or four a day, from ministries in urgent need. Then a man raising his support calls and wants to drop by for an hour to solicit financial backing. After him follows a brother in dire straits who wants an extra 500 dollars for unexpected ministry expenses. Driving across town one sees a billboard with a toll-free number appealing for money to be used in famine relief in Africa. A young college student is raising funds to go to the islands for two weeks of carpentry service. An elderly man wants to spend 900 dollars to deliver personally 200 dollars worth of library books for a mission post library. And he is wanting me to share the excitement of his mission venture. Then I go home and turn the television on and it's money again from just about every angle. A para-church ministry has asked the church for support funds and we've granted it. Then they turn around and ask every individual in the fellowship for funds too. Then a family lets you know they are in financial bondage and their solution is to quit giving. Another person lets you know he does not like you any more, so, to get back at you, he quits giving to the church. Then you give fifty dollars to a poor, down-and-out drifter who tearfully pleads for help, and thirty minutes later happen to see him coming out of the liquor store. And next it's the phone ringing with someone wanting you to speak at a fundraiser for their cause.

That's when you feel like quitting.

Giving, you see, is hard work. And it's fraught with all manner of pitfalls and frustrations.

Just this month I sat beside a wealthy Christian businessman in a fund raiser banquet. We were discussing giving to Jesus Christ's work and he made an astute observation, saying, "I've found that it is harder to give money away benevolently than it is to earn it." And it is certainly true. In ministry there is so much waste, ineffectiveness, duplication, and misrepresentation. Trying to sort it all out and be involved in the genuine work of Christ is no easy task. But we mustn't quit. And we must not lose the zeal and joy and privilege of giving.

I remind you that in the early church, as with this church, when a person was excommunicated he was stripped of his right to give. How would that make you feel? What if today you were told, "You can't give any more." Would you miss anything significant? Let's look in the Bible and see.

In Proverbs 22:9 we're told, "A generous man will himself be blessed." What is the blessing of giving?

In the New Testament the authors are very specific about giving. But they never wear out the subject by overusing any one word. In fact, there are at least ten different words they used for financial offerings. And each word is ripe with insight into the experience of giving.

Loggia

In Matthew 5:47 Jesus asks his disciples, "What more are you doing than others?" The Greek word for "doing more than others" is *loggia* and it means "an extra collection." It is the opposite of a tax which one has to pay. It is an offering beyond all obligation. It is something one gives because he wants to.

Each of us, you see, pays taxes which provide much ministry by way of the fire department, the police, welfare, the public school system, national defense, foreign aid, and the like. Many of us even give to the United Way, the Lion's Club benefit, scouting, and the school orchestra. The loggia is a gift beyond Caesar. It is a gift beyond American citizenship. It is a gift reflecting our citizenship in the kingdom of God.

Charis

In 1 Corinthians 16:3 Paul speaks of giving, saying, "And when I arrive, I will send those whom you accredit by letter to carry your gift to Jerusalem." The Greek word for gift here is *charis* and it means grace or unearned love.

The whole idea behind this is that God will pour out his love and provision in our lives that we in turn might pour it out to others who will join us in glorifying God. This notion is foreign to the American work ethic which says, "Work so you may have!" The charismatic work ethic Paul is talking about here says, "Work so you may have so you may help others." And that is exactly what the Corinthian Christians were doing — giving money to the relief of Christians in Jerusalem who were suffering through a famine.

I admit I've had to learn much about this in the past four years. You see, I used to see the church as a kind of water bucket from which we handed cups of cool water ministry to others. And since there was only so much water in the bucket, we had to be careful how we gave it out. After all, there was a limit to what we could do!

But no more! I'm coming to affirm the church as more of a pipe connected to God, the possessor of indepletable resources on the one end and pouring out to a needy world on the other. And since God's supply is inexhaustible, there is no end to the blessings that can flow through us to others just as long as we've a good connection to God and allow no blockage in us.

Koinonia

In Romans 15:6 Paul says about giving "that together you may with one voice glorify the God and Father of our Lord Jesus Christ." And in 2 Corinthians 8:4 he mentions "begging us earnestly for the favor of taking part in the relief of the saints." The word used in both these passages is *koinonia* or fellowship. The idea is that we are not a bunch of individuals all out funding and fighting our own wars for personal glory. Rather, we are a unit, a team, an

55

army, a body of Christ pooling our time, talents, and resources for commonly embraced goals for the glory of Christ and his bride, the church.

When David went off to fight the Amalekites in 1 Samuel 30, the spoils of victory were divided among the soldiers who fought as well as with those who stayed home to watch the baggage. David understood that it was a team effort. And we must mature in our thinking as well. Each time we send a missionary out here, do we not make a covenant with them, saying, "You take this end of the rope and go down into the darkness and bring the light. We will stay here and hold the other end of the rope and pray for you and see that your supply needs are met." We are a body, a community of giving. We speak with one voice, with one koinonia of giving.

Diakonia

In 2 Corinthians 9:12 Paul speaks of giving with these words, "For the rendering of this service not only supplies the wants of the saints, but also overflows in many thanksgivings to God." The word here for "supplies the wants of the saints" is *diakonia* from which we get the word deacon. It means practical Christian service.

One of the fascinating things about money is that it can go where we can't go and do for Christ what we can't do. For instance, in the past year the body with one voice has given several thousand dollars to Christian famine relief and agricultural projects in Africa and Haiti. There's not a one of us who could go to these places and do much about it. But our money went. And it enabled people who could go and who could do something about it to minister. And the text promises that such diakonia giving would result in "overflowing thanksgiving to God."

A few years ago I was riding an elevator in a hotel. A young foreign student was on board too and I introduced myself and asked him where he was from. "Pakistan," he told me. But now he was a student medical intern in this country. His desire was to go back and minister to his countrymen as a Christian doctor. I asked him how he'd become a Christian and he told me about a Christian relief ministry that had come to his city after a terrible war. They had fed, clothed, and sheltered him and shared Christ with him, and now his life was overflowing with thanksgiving. And that is exactly how the Bible promised it would be!

Hadrotes

In 2 Corinthians 8:20 Paul writes, "We intend that no one should blame us about this liberal gift which we are administering." The word for "liberal gift we are administering" is *hadrotes* and it means abundance.

The notion here is that God will meet our needs and give us a surplus, even beyond ten percent, that we can give away to others.

You can see this type of giving in the book of Ruth. Ruth and Naomi are widows down on their luck looking for their next meal and a new start in life. Boaz is a wealthy farmer busily harvesting his crops. Faithful to God's laws he does not reap his field border to border nor does he pick up what is dropped by accident. Such extras are for the poor to scavenge. And Ruth is one of them. Well, you remember how Boaz is generous with Ruth. They fall in love. And not only is Ruth given a new start in life, Boaz is too as they marry and become part of the ancestry of Jesus Christ.

"Hadrotes" or "abundance" means that we won't live border to border and off every scrap of our incomes. It means we shall set a standard of living well inside our resources so that we can be free and open handed with those God brings into our lives as well. And who knows what love stories await us out there as well!

Eulogia

Second Corinthians 9:5 says, "So I thought it necessary to urge the brethren to go on to you before me, and arrange in advance for this gift you have promised so that it may be ready not as an exaction but as a willing gift." The word here for gift is *eulogia* and it means bounty. It means that God will put so much in our midst that we'll have to break out of here with most of it or we'll be crushed under the weight of it all.

The vision God has given us is to make the church here like a ship knifing through the sea. She is on course, battle ready, and fully stocked. Quite often divers put on their diving suits and jump off the ship into the dark undersea world to bring the light of the gospel to those submerged in sin. We aship hold their lifelines and pump the air to them and haul them in when they've been down long enough.

This past year people have jumped off into prison ministry and we've bought the Bibles and books they've taken with them. We've funded music ministry in schools, poor churches, and orphanages. We've printed the truth God is showing us here and put it in mail-outs, newspapers, and magazines — over 2,400,000 pieces in the last year! Our elders have gone out to teach at conferences, colleges, rest homes, other churches, and beyond. And better still, the members here, right where you live, are loving and sharing Christ with their neighbors in a lifestyle of ministry.

We are not hoarding our blessings and strangling on too much. We are busily giving it away as fast as God gives it to us beyond our basic needs.

Leitourgia

Second Corinthians 9:12 talks about giving as "the rendering of this service." And the Greek word here is *leitourgia* from which we get our English word liturgy. It basically means service. The idea behind it is that of a service voluntarily accepted for the benefit of the nation. For instance, a citizen might take it upon himself to outfit an army for the defense of his nation. He didn't have to do so. He simply did it because he wanted to.

We do this today when we see that the rent is paid, the phone bill is up to date, the lights on, and a staff in place. We do it when we fund and encourage seminary studies, missions conferences, campus Bible studies, marriage conferences, and Sunday school. We do it overall as we see that what it takes to "equip the saints for the work of the ministry" is in place and on time.

Alms

In Acts 24:17 Paul admits, "Now after some years I came to bring my nation alms." The word "alms" means rightness. It means to do the right thing with one's money at the appropriate time.

One can see this in the story of the good Samaritan. The blood-ied traveler was incorrectly passed up by several religious people.

But a traveling salesman opened his heart and hands and pocket-book to the victim. In short, he did the right thing. He fulfilled love's demands.

I love that cartoon that shows the Good Samaritan talking to the wounded traveler by the roadside. He's saying, "I can't stop and help you now because I'm on my way to a charismatic conference on healing. But when I return I'll have some great teaching tapes for you!" That is "wrongness." "Rightness" translates love and theology and talk into what it takes to bring the wounded victim to the inn and subsequent healing.

Prosphora

Acts 24:17 also uses the word *prosphora* for giving. Paul says, "Now after some years I came to bring to my nation alms and offerings."

The Greek word *prosphora* means sacrifices. The Old Testament idea of animal sacrifice is behind this giving. Jewish worshipers did not give the blind, deformed, runt of the flock. They gave the firstborn, the first fruits, the one without blemish.

I know for years I gave God the leftovers from my resources. After I'd paid all my bills, bought everything I wanted, traveled and played at whim, whatever was left I gave to Jesus. And there was rarely anything left.

I find, now, however, that when I make my offering first and give up something that is a sacrifice to part with, then there is enough left to buy food, pay the bills, and play with.

I like the way C. S. Lewis put it. "There should be a measure of hurt, a bit of sacrifice in our giving. I seek to give until it starts to hurt. Then I give a little more and I know I'm in keeping with what the Bible teaches about sacrifice." For us it might mean giving up another vacation or a trip home or a new wardrobe or new wallpaper in the kitchen just to see that our missionaries have what it takes to stay on the job. Again, in stewardship, the issue is not "How much of my money am I going to give to God?" but "How much of God's money am I going to keep for myself?"

Paratheike

In 2 Timothy 1:12 Paul uses the word *paratheike* for giving, saying, "God is able to keep that which I have committed unto him against that day." A paratheike was a kind of deposit one put in the temple bank for safekeeping. It was something given to another to guard for them. And Paul is saying that what we give to the work of Jesus Christ is safely deposited with God. It's just like what Jesus said in Matthew 6:19-21: "Do not lay up for yourselves treasures on earth, where moth and rust consume and where thieves break in and steal, but lay up for yourselves treasures in heaven, where neither moth nor rust consume and where thieves do not break in and steal. For where your treasure is, there will your heart be also."

Did you hear about the two men climbing a mountain? They came to a difficult cliff and one man said, "I can't make it up there!" The other man didn't say anything. He just reached in his friend's back pocket, grabbed his wallet, and quickly threw it to the ledge atop the cliff. And in two minutes his friend had climbed up there to get it. Where our treasure is there also are our heart and hands and feet and mouth! And Jesus and Paul are reminding us that our treasure should be beyond this world, deposited safely with God.

Conclusion

What if we quit giving? What if God and the church denied us our privilege to give? Indeed, that would be a miserable turn of events! And in ten ways and more our lives would be impoverished, not to mention those who are on the receiving end of our ministry giving!

So, in the midst of all the immaturity, the begging, the waste, the constant appeals, let's not lose sight of the privilege we have to give to Jesus as he's given to us and see his kingdom grow among us and throughout the whole wide world.

I for one do not want to forget that these ten meanings of giving are all mine to give! After all, no one has taken away my right to give. And I'm surely not going to take it away myself.

I remind you that the church is God's idea. She is not a substitute we've put in her place and asked God to bless. I remind you that giving is a part of our covenant vows together here. I remind you to give motivated by love, to give joyously, and to give as the Holy Spirit leads you.

As is our custom here, each of us is to go home and seek the Holy Spirit, asking him to put in our hearts and minds a figure he wants us to give regularly. When you think you've arrived at that figure, check it out to see if it represents a loving sacrifice for Christ. Then, when you've settled it, simply trust Christ to give it to you to give. And together we'll get on with the work of Jesus! For him and his are all ours to give!

The Channel
Between The Buoys

Proverbs 1:20-33

"Let's go boating!"

How I love to hear those words! It means open sky, shore
birds, negotiating the chop on the sea, perhaps a water-borne adventure out to Bald Head Island!

I must confess I'm new at nautical adventures. I've shown my
ignorance by running out of gas, falling overboard, even running
aground.

Mishaps don't have to happen very often before one begins
to learn fast. For instance, I'm learning to read buoys, channel
markers, even the color of the water — all signs of where safe
passage lies.

Believe-you-me, the fun goes out of a boating trip quickly when
you run aground and have to wait six hours for the tide to change.
The mosquitoes and sun are glad for your flesh. But they're the
only ones.

So, a boatman can learn the hard way or he can learn to read
the buoys others passing before him have left.

Such is life in the broader sense. For there are but two ways to
learn. One may learn from God and others gone before. Or one
may learn everything on his own, the hard way.

The Book of Proverbs is a book of buoys marking out the
safe channels of life. It represents the ripened wisdom of many
generations.

"Wisdom" in the Hebrew language is *chokmah*. A hard to trans-
late word, wisdom vaguely means the ability to meet each challenge put before you so as to get the best results.

No generation wants wisdom uncultivated. And, gladly, the Book of Proverbs is a rich deposit of wisdom. Indeed, it is the first book of wisdom literature known to humanity.

Proverbs was written primarily by King Solomon. But others before and after contributed also. It includes truisms, pithy sayings, folk wisdom, and advice memorably written as a guide to choice behavior. And when one internalizes it, Proverbs becomes an inner compass guiding one's behavior.

Here in the United States Ben Franklin, our 1776 elder statesman from Pennsylvania, wrote and collected wisdom literature in *The Sayings of Poor Richard.* "A stitch in time saves nine." "The early bird catches the worm." But, alas, Franklin's wisdom literature was only "this-worldly" and not "other-worldly," too. Hence, it left God out of the human endeavor. Proverbs in the Old Testament is both earthly and heavenly. And, as such, it gives advice on sex, work, loans, speech, anger, marriage, criticism, humor, and so much more!

Check out the text, Proverbs 1:20-33. Wisdom is likened to a woman walking the streets crying out for men to draw near. To the ancient reader, this, indeed, was a shocking metaphor! A lady of breeding stayed home. When she had to venture out it was always with a veil, hair put up, and with a chaperone. The idea of a lady walking the streets raising her voice in the market (v. 20), crying out on city walls (v. 21), and speaking to men at city gates (v. 21) was unthinkable.

Yet one sees here how very serious God is about making himself known among beggars, sellers, farm hands, criminals, and the well-to-do of every town.

Notice that Lady Wisdom walks among us and sees three sorts of people.

She spies the "simple" (v. 22). These are the untutored youths of society. Proverbs 1:4 says the entire book was written "that prudence may be given to the simple; knowledge and discretion to the youth."

Dame Wisdom also sees the scoffer on city streets. She asks, "How long will scoffers delight in their scoffing?" (v. 22). Psalm 1:1 speaks of persons who "sit in the seat of scoffers" rather than delight in God. They are interested in no one's advice but their own.

Third, our woman of wisdom sees fools. In Hebrew, literally, "fool" is *kesil*, those who "hate knowledge." They live for themselves, for today only.

To the simple, the scoffer, and the fools of every town wisdom "cries," "raises her voice" (v. 20), "speaks" (v. 21), "reproves," pours out her thoughts (v. 22). She stretches out her hands (v. 24), and she laughs and mocks (v. 26).

Do you sense her urgency in imparting wisdom for life? Wisdom knows if she is "ignored" (v. 25) people will fall into "calamity" (v. 26), panic will strike like a storm (v. 27), and people will "eat the fruit of their way" (v. 31). She even mentions untimely death (v. 32).

Ah, but the wise "will dwell secure" (v. 33).

In 1 Kings 3 God Almighty invited King Solomon to "ask what I shall give you" (v. 5). Solomon asked for wisdom as he went in and out among the people. And his petition pleased God in that Solomon did not ask for the usual — money, health, long life, the death of his enemies, and so on! So God granted Solomon wisdom — the ability to meet each challenge put before him so as to get the best results. And in finding wisdom Solomon also found long life, wealth, family, and even a life that outlived his enemies.

If you study Proverbs, the wisdom of Solomon, you'll find it 31 chapters long. There is a chapter for each day of the month. This book cries out to you; wisdom holds out her hands to you pleadingly. Will you turn aside to learn?

Queen
Of Hearts!

Proverbs 31:10-31

Sociologists have defined her. Psychologists have analyzed her. Pollsters have surveyed her. But here's what those who know her best — children — have to say.

Liz Ann, age 8. "Who is a mother? She knows what is important. This is why God asked her to be a mother."

Louise, age 7. "A mother is the only one if she sings your favorite song it stops thundering."

Jimmy, age 8. "A mommy is a wife. A mommy looks after children and she yells."

Gary, age 6. "A mother doesn't do anything except she wants to. Nobody makes her take baths and naps or takes her frog away."

Harry, age 8. "If I forget to tell my mom I need my shepherd costume tomorrow morning, she finds one in the night. That is a mother."

Laura, age 6. "Mothers are wonderful! She spends all her time on you. A mother is like God, except God is better."

As with these children, today's text is a celebration of the feminine and motherhood. And with Proverbs 31 we can etch the role of the woman in family a bit more deeply and accurately in our minds.

I've heard Proverbs 31 called the Statue of Liberty of Womanhood. My wife calls the Proverbs 31 lady "The Bionic Christian Woman." After all, she sells real estate, does lap work, is a cook, wife, mother, and directs a staff. Indeed, she is the Empress of Domestic Arts.

Today when motherhood is so avoided, when male and female roles are so confused, when the home is so frequently broken, when college Home Economics majors are a dying breed, so many women are asking, "How can I be the woman God wants me to be?" How can I be the wife my husband adores? My children need? My boss requires? My friends depend upon?

Other societies have been confused, too, over the role of women. Amazon women in South America cut off a breast so they could pull a bow. Feminists in North America abort their children so they can have a career or shapely figure or both. But the Bible shares the good news that no female need mutilate herself to be the right person. Just being yourself in Christ is enough!

The role model for women is Proverbs 31. Don't be intimidated by her. Simply imitate her.

True, the Proverbs 31 woman never really existed except in the mind of a queen. This Bible chapter is the childhood memory of Lemuel, a young prince. It was the wisdom his mother put there, a sort of composite ideal.

Attitude

First, consider the attitude this feminine role model has.

Likely she is not a beauty queen. In verse 30 her husband praised her character not her body. He minimized beauty and charm, saying, "Charm is deceitful, and beauty is vain, but a woman who fears the Lord is to be praised."

Today we emphasize too much a woman's looks, weight, hair, nails, and clothing. And we act as if character doesn't matter. We need to skim such ladies magazines as *Glamour, Vogue, Vanity*, and *Better Homes and Gardens* to see what I mean.

The result? We fix in our minds a view of womanhood that is both false and unreachable. So women are frustrated, angry, depressed, self-loathing, and anorexic.

The Bible tells us of Satan, the deceiver. He didn't like what God made him to be — a creature, limited, under God's authority. So he rebelled, trying to be someone he was not. And when I do not accept myself, my limits, I share in his rebellion.

The Proverbs 31 woman is self-accepting. She may not have had the glamour, but she had the character. Read the litany of her life. There were no "if only" games in her head. "If only I were richer ... If only I were prettier ... If only I had wed another man ... If only I had this ... If only I were like her!"

The Germans have a proverb: "We must carve our lives out of the wood we have." That's what God's woman does. No wishful comparisons. No unfair expectations. Like the character in the play *You're A Good Man, Charlie Brown!* she sings, "I'm awfully glad I'm me!" And she busies herself making the most of who she is in her family, town, and day with God.

In verse 21 she is "not afraid of the snow." Verse 25 mentions her dignity, laughter, and strength. Verse 18 mentions her business sense: "She perceives that her merchandise is profitable." Clearly her inner life matches what God thinks and expects of her.

I know a woman recently widowed. She's let herself go, is unkempt, smelly, and reclusive. "I have no one to look at me, to make me feel wanted anymore." She'd stopped caring for the outside because she didn't care for the inside. But the Proverbs 31 woman kept her inside attitude in tune with God and it made her outside most appealing.

Actions

Now, let's consider this role model's actions.

There are two types of people — givers and takers. Givers are creative, industrious servants, loving and nurturing. Takers are lazy, expect a handout, are selfish and lustful. Today, vast numbers of women are becoming takers.

Nowhere has this become more obvious than with abortion. Twenty-six percent of pregnancies in North Carolina are aborted. There's an abortion every 22 seconds in the United States. There were over one million infants slain last year in this nation. Why? Because women were living for their rights, not their responsibilities.

Indeed! Women have a right to choose to have sex or not. They have a right to choose conception control or not. But after a child is conceived no woman has a right to murder!

Where is the God-given maternal instinct today? It is crushed under the feet of the feminine self hell-bent on taking instead of giving. Hence Mother Teresa observed, "You are a destroyed nation. When you start killing your own children, what is left to destroy?"

The Proverbs 31 woman has children. "Her children rise up and call her blessed!" (v. 38).

The most God-like act of which one is capable is parenthood: to create with God, to love with God, to train with God, to suffer and sacrifice with God, to forgive with God. The woman of Proverbs 31 is properly in the middle of all this. She is a nurturer, clothing (v. 21), cooking (v. 15), training (vv. 2-5), and even helping a son find a suitable wife (v. 10).

She's not ingrown nor "cocooned" with just her family. Verse 20 speaks of her helping the poor. She is kind (v. 26). And she is even an economic force in the city, selling girdles, planting fields, and selling real estate (vv. 16, 24).

Yes, there are givers and takers. But our holy madam is a giver. She loves herself. But she also loves her neighbor.

Characteristics

Let us now examine her characteristics.

Verses 10-31 extol her as a commendable wife and mother, family-centered, industrious, self-disciplined, orderly, a shrewd businesswoman, refined of taste, manifesting grace and hospitality, charitable with the needy, deeply respectful of God. Wow! What a mouthful!

A divorce lawyer recently figured out the monetary value of a homemaker. A woman in such a role is chauffeur, gardener, family counselor, nanny, cleaning woman, bookkeeper, seamstress, cook, dishwasher, nurse, tutor, and more. This attorney calculated 40,823.64 dollars a year, or 785.07 dollars a week. Indeed, the value of a good wife has long been known. Verse 10 says she is "more precious than rubies."

I like the cartoon of a boy looking at his mom's wedding picture and asking, "Is that the day you came to work for us?" Yes, ladies, it starts when you sink into his arms! It ends with your arms in the sink.

But notice carefully. The Proverbs 31 lady is not motivated by pay. Nor is she afraid of her husband. Why does she get up so early to cook? Why does she stay up late sewing? Verse 30 says she fears God. She is awed by the Almighty. He is her motivation.

Isn't it interesting that she trusts in God. So she takes on God's characteristics. Verses 11-12 say of her, "The heart of her husband trusts in her. She does him good *all* the days of her life."

If your *oven* worked nine out of ten times, would you have it? If your car worked every day but Fridays would you keep it? Of course not! And our empress of the domestic scene, Mrs. Proverbs 31, is steadfast. She is so daily. There is no lapse in her.

Not all women are like this. Proverbs 12:4 says, "A good wife is the crown of her husband. But she who brings shame is like rottenness in his bones."

The interesting thing about trusting God is that it makes us trustworthy. The "fruit of the Spirit is ... faithfulness" (Galatians 5). And this trust also leads us to trust others. Note in the text how this woman does it all. She delegates. "She provides tasks for her maidens" (v. 15). She gives responsibility away, to her children and to her helpers.

She's not cynical. She believes in God and his people.

Conclusion

Reduce this laudable woman to her basics in attitude, action, and characteristics and you get someone living the great commandment. She loves God, and she loves her neighbor as herself (Mark 12:28-31).

And how important are such mothers? A few years ago my wife was out shopping. I was home with my three children. My middle son, age twelve, walked in, saw mom was missing, and said, "Where is everybody?"

Where are the mothers of this generation? Where are those givers who'll love God, self, husband, children, and town?

Will you ask God to make you such a woman? For indeed, such feminine ideals are not made of earthly strivings. They are built by the divine!

Mirror, Mirror On The Wall...!

Esther 7:1-6, 9-10; 9:20-22

Do you remember the fairy tale "Snow White"? Recall how the wicked witch peered into her magic looking glass and said, "Mirror, mirror, on the wall, who is the fairest of them all?"

The mirror's answer was quite disappointing. "It's certainly not you, Ugly!"

Does your mirror ever do that to you? Sad to say, but thousands of people's mirrors disappoint them each day.

Have you ever known someone to look at a photograph of himself in his high school yearbook and say, "Golly, I take an awful picture. Just look at me!" Have you ever known a woman overinterested in clothes and make-up? She is always shopping, always touching up her make-up, and always trying to decide which tint to color her hair. Certainly you've run into people with inferiority complexes. "I can't do anything right!" They say as they mope through life gloomily. And drugs? Why, if one does not like his neighbor he can move. But if you don't like yourself, where can you go to get away from self? For many the answer comes in alcohol and drugs, a form of chemical escape. Then there is that strange man. He was so nice, but you found out he became a transvestite, moved to another city and changed his name from Robert to Roberta. And what about your friend at the club? He shot and killed himself last month. Why suicide?

All of these people are manifesting a brokenness that has troubled the human race since the fall. The book of Genesis teaches that man once had a good self-esteem. Both Adam and Eve were naked and "unashamed" (Genesis 3:7). They accepted who they were. God has looked on all his creation and pronounced it very good. And they looked on themselves and agreed.

But then came the fall. Both Adam and Eve disobeyed the Lord. And the result, as we have seen, was devastating. The fall broke man. It broke him utterly. And one of the first ways Adam and Eve found themselves broken was in their self-image. No longer were they accepting toward their bodies. They became alarmed at their appearance. And so they clothed themselves with fig leaves. Gone was their self-assurance. Missing was their self-worth.

This break is still within us today. And one's inability to love himself affects nearly every area of his life. It affects one's relationship with God. If you hate yourself, it is impossible to love the Lord. The logic usually runs like this: "I don't like me. And God is my creator. Therefore, I will have nothing more to do with God. He messed me up the first time. I won't give him a chance to foul me up again!"

Low self-esteem can also adversely affect your family life. A teenager who has difficulty with self-love might begin to overdress and run up some high clothing bills. Or she might begin to "underdress." Her dad begins to notice and complains, "You're not going to school dressed like that, are you?"

Self-loathing can also affect your friendships. Who wants to be around a fellow who has a dark cloud of inferiority hanging over his head all the time? Misery loves company, but company doesn't love misery.

Self-confidence could get you a promotion, while personal contempt never will.

And finally, even one's elderly years can be spoiled by inner reproach. We see this in the fear of aging, unwillingness to accept the limitations of advanced years, and in senior citizens who try to be something they are not.

In the great commandment we are told to love ourselves. And as we have seen, in Legion's life, God's salvation helps restore our self-regard. If you study through the Scriptures you will begin to see just how a man can learn to prize himself as highly as the Lord does.

Your Looks Are No Accident

One of the first facts one needs to learn about loving himself is that his body is no mistake. God prescribed exactly how we look.

Did you hear about the child who went to the zoo, came home and wrote a letter to God? "Dear God," the boy wrote, "did you mean for a giraffe to look like that or was it an accident?" A lot of people feel that way about themselves. "There really must be some mistake! My neck shouldn't be this long!" "Me and my big feet!" "Wow! Look at my face! Ugly! When God was handing out looks, I must have thought he said 'books' and hid behind the door because I didn't want any."

But did you know that the Bible teaches that God is in complete control of creation? You are no accident, no freak of nature! Just listen to what the psalmist had to testify as he examined himself in the mirror:

For thou didst form my inward parts,
thou didst knit me together in my mother's womb.
I praise thee, for thou art fearful and wonderful.
Wonderful are thy works!
Thou knowest me right well; my frame was not hidden
    from thee,
when I was being made in secret,
intricately wrought in the depths of the earth.
Thy eyes beheld my unformed substance;
in thy book were written, every one of them,
the days that were formed for me,
when as yet there was none of them.
— Psalm 139:13-16

God has known you since conception, and before. He knit you together. He formed your sex, your race, even your mind and your face! You are no accident! You are the workmanship of God.

You must know that when the Lord made you he made you with features, some of which are changeable and some of which are unchangeable. An unchangeable feature would be your race, the intelligence quotient of your mind, the size of your foot, perhaps even the shape of your head or the texture of your hair. The Bible makes it clear that it is a sin to try to change some unchangeable features about yourself. A transvestite does this when he attempts to alter his sex. A teenager might sin in this way if he tried to pretend he was really older than he was. In Leviticus 19:28, God even forbids us to mutilate our bodies with ornate scars and tattooing. There are, however, changeable features about our bodies. And it is here that the Lord allows us to make improvements. Your weight is usually a changeable feature. So is your smile, and the twinkle in your eyes. With the gift of science God has even allowed us to straighten teeth, improve our complexions with better hygiene, and even straighten a nose or minimize a scar by plastic surgery. If you can afford such care, these things are changeable. And it is no sin to try to make oneself as attractive as possible.

Designed To Serve A Purpose

Not only does the Bible point out that the Lord prescribed how you look, it also teaches that God designed you with a specific purpose in mind. He made you with certain abilities and even disabilities so that you could accomplish his plans for your life. You can see this in Acts 9:15 where God called the apostle Paul to serve him and refers to the man as "a chosen instrument of mine." The word "instrument" is the same as "tool." You see, God had a job to do, and he reached for Paul just like we reach for a screwdriver or a hammer instead of a pair of pliers or scissors. God had made Paul for a specific purpose.

I was in a sawmill one day. The whole plant had been shut down for two days due to a breakdown. A mechanic showed me an odd-shaped cog covered with grease. "This is the culprit," he said. "It cracked and ruined the whole system." After finding an exact replacement, the machinery began to run once more. But all it took was one ugly and dirty little part that quit doing its job and the entire plant was shut down! Creation is like that, too. It takes all kinds! Each of us is designed by God to fill a job here on earth. And the Lord, seeing how he wants us to fit in, designed us with all we need to achieve his goals. We are unique! Oh, we may feel like we're that small, grease-covered cog, but let us stop doing our job and things go amuck. Stop and think! You're the only one of your kind. No one else has your fingerprints. God made you especially for a purpose. And in some special way, you complete the universe!

Saint Paul is interesting to study in this light. This apostle was probably short. His real name was Saul. But someone had nicknamed him Paul, which is Latin for "Shorty." We are told that Paul was not a good speaker. His sermons were weak. And, as if these "drawbacks" were not enough, Paul had also been shipwrecked two or three times, he had been whipped with a cat-o'-nine-tails, rejected by his own kinsmen, and even stoned. Imagine the gashes! No doctor had stitched him up! The wounds must have healed as frightful disfigurements. And then there was the "thorn in the flesh." Was it a problem with his eyes? Perhaps. A doctor named Luke was at Paul's side much of the time. Paul must have been something of a walking candidate for the hospital emergency room. But instead of being hospitalized, Paul was often imprisoned. Yet God took this weak man, a tent-maker by trade, and made him the first great missionary of the Christian faith and author of half of the New Testament.

You see, Paul's body was all a part of God's plan. Paul did not choose it, but God chose him for it. Paul prayed for a "better" body, but God said, "No." He said, "My grace is sufficient for you, for my power is made perfect in weakness" (2 Corinthians 12:9).

The truth is that the Lord gives each of us the talents, opportunities, and limitations we need to fit into his plan and achieve his goals for our lives. The problem comes when we do not accept that which we are. We grumble because we were born too late, too short to be a basketball star, too homely to be a movie starlet, or too slow mentally to be a doctor. In a *Peanuts* cartoon, Charlie Brown is unhappy about his lot in life. Lucy is bugging him. She follows him around, saying, "You're a nerd, Charlie Brown! You are a real zero. You'll never amount to anything!" Finally, little Charlie yells, "Stop it! Stop it! Stop it! Don't bother me anymore. I didn't get a chance to fill in an application to be me!" That's right! None of us got to choose our looks, our limitations, and our gifts. It is mostly thrust on us like it was on Paul. For we, too, are "chosen instruments" of God to carry out the Lord's work (Acts 9:15). Right here is where we are faced with a choice. We can either accept ourselves and cooperate with God in achieving his goals, or we can hate what he made us and put our hands to some other task. The Bible warns us to take the former choice. Isaiah 45:9-11 says:

> Woe to him who strives with his maker,
> an earthen vessel with the potter!
> Does the clay say to him who fashions it,
> "What are you making?" or "Your work has no
>   handles"?
> ... Thus says the Lord,
> "Will you question me about my children, or command
>   me
> concerning the work of my hands?"

Unless one wants to strive against his maker and suffer "woe," one has to accept himself. And here is where the Christian faith can be helpful. God is a benevolent Lord. We are special to him. As such, can we not trust him with our looks? Perhaps God saw that giving us great beauty would have made us vain and cause us to miss his plan. So, out of love, he made our looks more commonplace. Perhaps God saw that great intelligence would not be necessary in our job. Maybe he saw that short stature or a fair complexion would be necessary in accomplishing his goals. Whatever the case may be, the Bible teaches that we are no mistake. God designed how we look. And God saw that making us this way was necessary in achieving his goals for our lives.

Queen Esther is fascinating to study here. A Jewish woman exiled from her homeland, conscripted to live in a pagan king's harem, she puts herself in harm's way to save her people from a holocaust. Of her looks, talents, strategic placement, and opportunity, Mordecai says, "And who knows whether you have not come to the kingdom for such a time as this?" Hear that? It is true of you as well. God gave you as a gift, a servant, a minister in your time and place.

Still On The Easel!
Another important word of Scripture is this. God is not finished making us yet. Ephesians 2:10 says, "We are his workmanship, created in Christ Jesus for good works, which God prepared
beforehand that we should walk in them." It is fascinating to note
that the Greek word used here for "workmanship" is *poema* from
which we get our English word "poem." Notice also that it doesn't
say, "We *were* his workmanship," past tense. It says, "We are!"
Right now God is still working on us.

Have you ever seen that famous unfinished portrait of George
Washington by Gilbert Stuart? It hangs in a Boston museum, but
copies of it are familiar to every school child. The picture is considered a masterpiece, yet it has never been completed. The artist
died before he finished it. Our lives are like that painting. We are
unfinished. But our Lord is not dead. He is still on the job. We are
still up on his easel! Work is underway. And we are literally Christians under construction. I like the way the apostle Paul put it in 2
Corinthians 3:18. "We are being changed into his likeness from
one degree of glory to another, for this comes from the Lord who is
the Spirit."

This gives us great hope! If you do not like what you are, just
wait until tomorrow. The Lord is not through with you yet. In him
you are being changed, improved. I saw a button on a Christian
the other day. It said, "PBPWM. GNFWMY!" When I inquired
as to its meaning, I was told that the letters stood for the sentences,
"Please be patient with me. God's not finished with me yet!"

The Frame Around The Character
The Bible also teaches that we should learn to see our bodies
as picture frames. They are frames around inner qualities which
God wants to develop. Now you will notice that the purpose of a
picture frame is to draw your eye into the painting itself. If a frame
is too gaudy, it calls attention to itself instead of the picture. Likewise our physical bodies are not an end in themselves. They are
like frames. They should draw attention to the character within.

Listen to what 1 Peter 3:3-4 says about this: "Let not yours be
the outward adorning with braiding of hair, decoration of gold, and

wearing of robes, but let it be the hidden person of the heart with the imperishable jewel of a gentle and quiet spirit, which in God's sight is very precious." We seem to be doing the opposite of this in western society today. The emphasis now is on outward glamor, physical beauty. You have seen a body beauty pageant. But have you ever seen a character beauty pageant? People want sex appeal toothpaste, eye-catching hairstyles, shapely bodies, and style-of-the-minute clothing. Now don't get me wrong! I am not against physical beauty. I think a Christian should try to look as pleasing as possible. What I am saying is that character is more important than physical glamor. Character lasts. Physical beauty does not.

Esther was, indeed, a beauty queen. But she had the character to match it. She approached the king with courage yet a gentle and quiet spirit.

An elderly lady, crippled by arthritis, asked her visiting pastor, "Why does God let us get old? Why do we have to hurt so?" The minister shook his head, "I'm not sure," he said, "but I have a theory. I think the Lord has given physical strength and beauty to the young because that's the only kind of beauty they can have. But the strength and beauty of age is spiritual. It is character. It is wisdom. We gradually lose the physical beauty that is temporary so we will be certain to concentrate on the beauty that lasts, spiritual character!" This is true. "God," the Bible says in 1 Samuel 16:7, "sees not as man sees; man looks on the outward appearance, but the Lord looks on the heart." God is not as concerned with what we look like on the outside as he is with what we are on the inside. If it were up to man, we would bother only with outward glamor. But God takes this away from us. Physical beauty, if indeed we ever had it, fades rapidly. If you don't believe me, return to your class reunion! But the Lord has a plan in all this. He takes something away from us to give us something better. He takes something perishable away from us to give us something imperishable. Our physical beauty fades so that we will learn to concentrate on character. The purpose of aging is to make us concentrate on the picture and not on the frame.

God in his goodness has not left us to fend for ourselves in building character. He has given us the Holy Spirit whose sole purpose is to reproduce Christ's character within us. He is ministering within, assisting us to "put on the new nature, which is being renewed ... after the image of its creator" (Colossians 3:10). If you had William Shakespeare inside you, you could write some fine plays. If Winston Churchill could live in you, what speeches you could make! If T. S. Eliot could live in you, the world would see excellent poetry from your pen. If Rembrandt could live in your heart, you could paint a masterpiece! But, alas, these geniuses are all dead. Not one of them can live within you. But there is one genius, one master, who is still alive. He can live inside you! The man is Jesus Christ! He can put his Spirit within you. He can empower you with his love, his character. It can all be reproduced in your life!

I know many people who are not very becoming physically. Many of their physical features might be considered handicaps. Some are short and have big noses. Others are tall and skinny. Some even have had burn scars from accidents. For the most part their "drawbacks" are unchangeable features. From the world's point of view, they should be bitter, reclusive, and full of self-image troubles. But no! These are some of the most refreshing people I know! They have joy. They have sincerity. In their lives are deep reservoirs of love. And they are wise. You hardly even notice their bodies, for upon meeting them you are drawn right into their very souls.

One man I know, an airline pilot, suffered terrible disfiguring burns over ninety percent of his body when his plane crashed. "I look like God wants me to look right now," he says, accepting his scars as for the moment, unchangeable. Yet behind all that ugly scar tissue there is something beautiful. He shimmers! His eyes twinkle! His voice is full of calm assurance. And God is using this fellow in some exciting ways among the paraplegic, the burned, and the scarred.

You Are A Testimony!

Not only does Scripture teach that our looks are prescribed by God and that we are made this way for a purpose. It also teaches that the Lord is not through with us yet. We are his poems, his

81

works of art! And he is working within us by the power of the Holy Spirit to reproduce Christ's character, to make us like Jesus. God does this for a purpose. It is advertisement. When we develop Christ's character, people will look at us and praise the artist who made us thus. Check this out with Matthew 5:16. Jesus said, "Let your light so shine before men, *that they may see your good works*" (not your *good looks*) "*and give glory to your Father who is in heaven.*"

Esther was God's embodiment of truth like this to the king and society in her day. She not only saved the Jews from a pogram, she proclaimed their God as well!

I was touring the National Gallery of Art in Washington once when I stopped to admire Murillo's painting of the return of the prodigal son. The picture was fascinating. On one canvas the artist seemed to have captured all of the joy, the excitement, the tender pain, and great spiritual longing of a long overdue embrace. As I stood admiring the masterpiece, a young couple strode up and gazed at the painting in silence. Finally the girl whispered, "Beautiful." "I agree," the man said. Then both together bent over to read the artist's signature. The same thing happens when the public is exposed to the character of Christ reproduced in our lives. They want to know what or who is responsible for the love, joy, peace, patience, gentleness, and wisdom in us. And, of course, their inquiry leads them to the Master himself, Christ Jesus.

A New Relationship With Your Designer?

Perhaps you are struggling with self-esteem. Maybe you find it difficult to accept yourself. Others have been there, too. The man Legion bruised himself with stones (Mark 5:5). King Saul committed suicide (1 Samuel 31:4). Even Martin Luther, the great church reformer, struggled with dire feelings of self-loathing. It is said that Luther used to abuse himself physically, demand more of his body than it could deliver. He was always down in the mouth, sour toward himself. This went on for years! Then one day, while Luther was studying his face in the mirror, a verse of Scripture from Galatians 2:20 came to mind, "I have been crucified with Christ; it is no longer I who live but Christ who lives in me; and the life I now live in the flesh I live by faith in the Son of God, who loved me and gave himself for me." With this thought in mind, Luther stiffened for a moment, thought, then said, "If Christ can love me and live in me, then there must be something lovable about me!" From that point on Martin Luther began not only to love God and his neighbor, he also began to love himself. The cross became a divine plus-mark on his life. Luther began to celebrate himself as the pearl of great price God sold all to buy.

You, too, with God's help can learn to love yourself. Go look in the mirror. Saint Augustine wrote, "Men go abroad to wonder at the height of mountains, at the huge waves of the sea, at the vast compass of the ocean, at the circular motion of the stars, and they pass by themselves without wondering." Why, the wonder of it all! You are made in the image of God! And what more beautiful image is there? You're so special that Christ died for you. You're the only one of your kind! So, why not thank God for making you what you are so far? Ask Jesus to save you, to put his marvelous Holy Spirit within you. Then put yourself back up on God's work-table and let him finish what he's started. "And I am sure that he who began a good work in you will bring it to completion at the day of Jesus Christ" (Philippians 1:6).

Mirror, mirror on the wall, who is the fairest of them all?

It is you, your life in Jesus, a work of art!

Lectionary Preaching After Pentecost

The following index will aid the user of this book in matching the correct Sunday with the appropriate text during Pentecost. All texts in this book are from the series for Lesson One, Revised Common Lectionary. (Note that the ELCA division of Lutheranism is now following the Revised Common Lectionary.) The Lutheran and Roman Catholic designations indicate days comparable to Sundays on which Revised Common Lectionary Propers are used.

(Fixed dates do not pertain to Lutheran Lectionary)

Fixed Date Lectionaries *Revised Common (including ELCA) and Roman Catholic*	**Lutheran Lectionary** *Lutheran*
The Day of Pentecost	The Day of Pentecost
The Holy Trinity	The Holy Trinity
May 29-June 4 — Proper 4, Ordinary Time 9	Pentecost 2
June 5-11 — Proper 5, Ordinary Time 10	Pentecost 3
June 12-18 — Proper 6, Ordinary Time 11	Pentecost 4
June 19-25 — Proper 7, Ordinary Time 12	Pentecost 5
June 26-July 2 — Proper 8, Ordinary Time 13	Pentecost 6
July 3-9 — Proper 9, Ordinary Time 14	Pentecost 7
July 10-16 — Proper 10, Ordinary Time 15	Pentecost 8
July 17-23 — Proper 11, Ordinary Time 16	Pentecost 9
July 24-30 — Proper 12, Ordinary Time 17	Pentecost 10
July 31-Aug. 6 — Proper 13, Ordinary Time 18	Pentecost 11
Aug. 7-13 — Proper 14, Ordinary Time 19	Pentecost 12
Aug. 14-20 — Proper 15, Ordinary Time 20	Pentecost 13
Aug. 21-27 — Proper 16, Ordinary Time 21	Pentecost 14
Aug. 28-Sept. 3 — Proper 17, Ordinary Time 22	Pentecost 15
Sept. 4-10 — Proper 18, Ordinary Time 23	Pentecost 16
Sept. 11-17 — Proper 19, Ordinary Time 24	Pentecost 17
Sept. 18-24 — Proper 20, Ordinary Time 25	Pentecost 18

Sept. 25-Oct. 1 — Proper 21, Ordinary Time 26	Pentecost 19
Oct. 2-8 — Proper 22, Ordinary Time 27	Pentecost 20
Oct. 9-15 — Proper 23, Ordinary Time 28	Pentecost 21
Oct. 16-22 — Proper 24, Ordinary Time 29	Pentecost 22
Oct. 23-29 — Proper 25, Ordinary Time 30	Pentecost 23
Oct. 30-Nov. 5 — Proper 26, Ordinary Time 31	Pentecost 24
Nov. 6-12 — Proper 27, Ordinary Time 32	Pentecost 25
Nov. 13-19 — Proper 28, Ordinary Time 33	Pentecost 26
	Pentecost 27
Nov. 20-26 — Christ the King	Christ the King

Reformation Day (or last Sunday in October) is October 31 (Revised Common, Lutheran)

All Saints' Day (or first Sunday in November) is November 1 (Revised Common, Lutheran, Roman Catholic)

Books In This Cycle B Series

GOSPEL SET
A God For This World
Sermons for Advent/Christmas/Epiphany
Maurice A. Fetty

The Culture Of Disbelief
Sermons For Lent/Easter
Donna E. Schaper

The Advocate
Sermons For Sundays After Pentecost (First Third)
Ron Lavin

Surviving In A Cordless World
Sermons For Sundays After Pentecost (Middle Third)
Lawrence H. Craig

Against The Grain — Words For A Politically Incorrect Church
Sermons For Sundays After Pentecost (Last Third)
Steven E. Albertin

FIRST LESSON SET
Defining Moments
Sermons For Advent/Christmas/Epiphany
William L. Self

From This Day Forward
Sermons For Lent/Easter
Paul W. Kummer

Out From The Ordinary
Sermons For Sundays After Pentecost (First Third)
Gary L. Carver

Wearing The Wind
Sermons For Sundays After Pentecost (Middle Third)
Stephen M. Crotts

Out Of The Whirlwind
Sermons For Sundays After Pentecost (Last Third)
John A. Stroman

SECOND LESSON SET
Humming Till The Music Returns
Sermons For Advent/Christmas/Epiphany
Wayne Brouwer

Ashes To Ascension
Sermons For Lent/Easter
John A. Stroman

www.ingramcontent.com/pod-product-compliance
Lightning Source LLC
Chambersburg PA
CBHW072013060426
42446CB00043B/2367